CHASE THE DEVIL

CHASE THE DEVIL

MURDER AND OBSESSION ON FLORIDA'S GULF COAST

TONY ADAME

ROWMAN & LITTLEFIELD
Lanham • Boulder • New York • London

Rowman & Littlefield
Bloomsbury Publishing Inc, 1385 Broadway, New York, NY 10018, USA
Bloomsbury Publishing Plc, 50 Bedford Square, London, WC1B 3DP, UK
Bloomsbury Publishing Ireland, 29 Earlsfort Terrace, Dublin 2, D02 AY28,
Ireland
www.rowman.com

British Library Cataloguing in Publication Information Available

Library of Congress Cataloging-in-Publication Data Available

ISBN 979-88-8180526-5 (cloth)
ISBN 979-88-8180527-2 (electronic)

For product safety related questions contact productsafety@bloomsbury.com.

∞™ The paper used in this publication meets the minimum requirements of
American National Standard for Information Sciences—Permanence of Paper
for Printed Library Materials, ANSI/NISO Z39.48-1992.

For Niko

To the living we owe respect; to the dead, we owe only the truth.

—Voltaire

CONTENTS

East Pensacola, 1985
Map courtesy Pensacola Police Department

❶

NEW YEAR'S EVE, 1984

New Year's Eve brought an unexpected storm out of the Gulf of Mexico, churning up over Pensacola Beach and Santa Rosa Island before it made landfall on the lush, sprawling bluffs on the western edge of Escambia Bay. The storm swallowed up the coastline in sheets of rain and a blanket of dense fog that stretched its fingers into Pensacola as the clock ticked toward the new year.

In a home just off the bluffs, Mary Lloyd watched the weather roll in from her front window as she went back and forth between her sick husband, Dr. James Lloyd, who was just starting to recover from a fever, and her sick dog, who seemed to be getting worse by the hour. Sometime past midnight, Mary found a number for an all-night veterinary clinic in the Yellow Pages and called to see if she could bring the dog in. She was told she could come in but not by herself, because the clinic was in a bad neighborhood; and if she did come, she needed to park facing the front of the clinic and flash her headlights twice before someone would come out to her and get the dog.

Mary's 19-year-old daughter, Sharon Edwards, returned home from a night of partying around 2 a.m. with her boyfriend, Jeffrey Pierce, and Mary asked them to come with her to the clinic almost as soon as they walked in the door. Tired from a night out, they refused initially then changed their minds within the hour when they realized how sick the dog was.

Edwards drove, and as she backed out of the driveway onto Peacock Drive, she pointed the headlights toward the empty lot across the street. The lot, overgrown with trees and bushes, was right next to Creighton Road, the neighborhood's main thoroughfare. In the neighborhood, the empty lot was mostly known as the place where one of their neighbors, Zuella Larson, left odd, oversized items next to the curb for trash pickup.

"Look, Mama," Edwards said as the car idled in the middle of the street. "Zuella threw out another mannequin."

In the headlights, through the rain and fog, Mary could see a young woman lying motionless in the dirt and grass just a few feet back from the road. She was on her left side, facing out toward the street, and her black-and-blue striped dress was pulled up over her face. She was naked from the chest down, barefoot, and her pantyhose were bunched up around one of her ankles. It looked like a pair of discarded blue panties were on the ground next to her head.

"That's not a mannequin," Mary said. "That's a girl."

Edwards crept the vehicle forward so the lights shone directly on the empty lot, and in an instant of realization and fear, she slammed her foot on the gas and the van sped away, careening off Peacock Drive and onto Creighton Road at breakneck speed. Mary waited a few seconds before she calmly told her daughter they needed to turn around. They needed to go home and call the police.

"It was terror ... just sheer terror," Mary would say later. "We're pulling into the driveway and running inside and even in those few minutes or seconds or however long it was you don't know if there's a killer waiting or walking around or just maybe watching and waiting for you to come home because they'd seen us drive by. It was the most scared I've ever been in my life."

Once inside, Edwards called the police and told them about the body. She said she and Pierce had not seen the woman's body when they drove by the empty lot shortly after 2 a.m., but the visibility through the rain and fog wasn't great, so there was a chance the body was already there and they didn't see it. Within minutes, the blue and red lights of a police car flashed outside their home, and Mary watched from the front window as a lone police officer got out of the car, flashlight in hand, and began to walk slowly toward the body.

* * *

Officer Ken Franks was a retired U.S. Navy veteran in his mid-30s when he joined the Pensacola Police Department in 1978 and became the oldest rookie cop in department history. On January 1, 1985, he was just months away from being promoted from patrol to investigations when he took the call from dispatch about a possible homicide on Peacock Drive. Upon his arrival, it was obvious to Franks the woman was already dead.

As he stood over the body with his flashlight, he could see her pantyhose pulled down, ripped and bunched around her left ankle. What Mary thought were panties on the ground by the woman's head was a light blue towel with blood on it. On one side of the woman's head, her hair was matted down with blood, and one of her arms had a large scrape across most of the forearm. Franks assumed this was from being dragged across the concrete. His first guess was she was in her late teens or early 20s. Franks knew the people who found the body were almost certainly watching through the front window of their home but didn't acknowledge them. He clocked a home directly across from the empty lot when he saw a light from inside the home flick on behind a thick row of camellia bushes.

Franks' first call was to Crime Scene Supervisor Bob Grant, who arrived within minutes. EMS personnel began to filter to Peacock Drive as Franks and Grant went back over the crime scene together, and it was in those few minutes that Grant made up his mind about not only who killed the young woman but how she'd been killed.

Without talking to anyone or consulting with any detectives, Grant believed he'd solved the case.

"The police came to the door, and we asked if we could leave and still take the dog to the vet," Mary said. "They said we couldn't go anywhere because the girl had been killed because we ran her over, which was ridiculous. They didn't want us to move our car because they thought there was evidence on it that showed my daughter had run over the girl and killed her. We didn't really have a choice at that point, so we just said 'OK, well, we didn't do it,' and had to wait inside. By the time they realized they were wrong, there were so many people out there that there was no way we were going to leave. We just did what we could to care for the dog ourselves ... and that dog lived for a long time, by the way."

Grant didn't abandon his "death by van" theory until more people began to show up at the crime scene and none of them saw things the way he did. To protect the woman's body from the rain, EMS covered it with a large white tarp that stretched out into the street, and Assistant Crime Scene Analyst Carolynn Stephens was called in. Even though she wasn't scheduled to work, she was filling in for several analysts who'd been out on New Year's Eve.

When lead investigator James Enterkin arrived around 6 a.m. and took charge, every major decision about the case from that moment forward went through him.

⚬ ⚬ ⚬

When Enterkin took stock of the crime scene, he saw things much differently than Grant did.

The first thing he noticed was thin red ligature marks around the victim's neck. This led him to believe the girl was strangled to death. Because she was partially nude, with her pantyhose ripped and bunched around one of her ankles, and her breasts and genitals seemed to have been left purposefully exposed, he thought it was likely she'd been sexually assaulted before she was killed. Because of where her body was left and the way it was left, his first instinct was that the strangulation, sexual assault and murder all occurred elsewhere. This was just the dump site.

Enterkin found a small cut on her head that was the source of the blood matting her hair down on one side. Here, he believed, she'd likely been struck with a large, hard object, and his best guess was a tire iron. Because of all the blood, he was almost certain she was still alive when she was struck, although the blow would not have been fatal but would have only served to either knock her unconscious or incapacitate her momentarily.

Franks stayed on past the scheduled end of his 12-hour shift to finish up his report then handed off patrol responsibilities to Officer Jerri Schadee around 9 a.m.; she went right into canvassing the neighborhood looking for anyone who may have seen or heard anything suspicious. Schadee, the first female officer in the history of the Pensacola Police Department, made a big impact in the one day she worked on the case by how thorough she was with door-to-door interviews.

Ralph Jordan, who lived one block from the empty lot, told Schadee he heard a vehicle with a loud muffler in the area around 3 a.m., going back and forth between Creighton Road and Scenic Highway several times. This was one block up from where the body was found. Two brothers who lived a few houses from the empty lot on Peacock Drive told Schadee they heard the same thing around the same time. Within a few hours, police found what they believed was the victim's black, size-10 high-heeled shoes discarded a few blocks west of the crime scene on Old Spanish Trail Road. Zuella Larson, the neighbor who sometimes left items for trash pickup in the empty lot, said her dogs began barking around 2:30 a.m. and then started barking again shortly before 4 a.m.

John Laabs lived next door to Mary and directly across from the empty lot on Peacock Drive in the home Franks spotted through the bushes after he initially approached the body. Laabs told Enterkin he took his dog outside to use the bathroom sometime around 3 a.m., and from a vantage point completely hidden by the bushes in his front yard, he watched a man and a woman argue for several minutes over the man wanting the woman to get into the car. He said it appeared she was holding her "panties or pantyhose," in her hand, and after a few minutes, she finally got in the car, and they drove off.

The police impounded a car left overnight on Peacock Drive after they determined it did not belong to anyone who lived on the street. They ruled the car out as part of the investigation after a woman came forward to say she'd left it there after she broke down around 3 a.m. and accepted a ride from a man who was driving by. The man who gave her a ride came to the scene after he saw a news report of a girl's body found on Peacock Drive. He said he'd seen the woman whose car broke down and convinced her to let him give her a ride home. She'd insisted on giving him a pair of men's jeans and a men's jean jacket she had in her car, which he showed to the police. Enterkin was certain this was the couple Laabs had seen.

Around 3 p.m., the Escambia County Sheriff's Office made an identification of the victim via a fingerprint match from a previous arrest. She was 23-year-old Tonya Ethridge McKinley — date of birth January 25, 1961 — and the address on her driver's license wasn't far from Peacock Drive. Enterkin took an officer with him to the listed address for Tonya, but no one answered the door, and neighbors said no one had lived there in quite some time. The second check on her driving record came back with a more recent address on Kelly Avenue, where Enterkin and the officer went next. These neighbors said Tonya lived there with a man named Tim Davidson and their infant son, Tim Davidson Jr., but she'd moved out sometime in the last few weeks. Neighbors also said the couple, who were both in their early 20s, was known for having frequent, explosive arguments that sometimes turned violent. Several of the neighbors said they'd seen Tim at home that morning.

Enterkin tracked down an address for Tonya's father, Joe Ethridge, who lived in Milton, a rural community about 30 minutes from Pensacola. Enterkin called the Santa Rosa County Sheriff's Office in Milton, and they dispatched several officers to deliver the death notice to her father. Public records checks on Tonya showed she was recently divorced from a man named Michael McKinley, which seemed to explain why she had the letter "M" tattooed on two knuckles on her left hand.

Around the same time as the sheriff's officer was delivering the death notice to Tonya's father, Tim Davidson called the Pensacola police "extremely agitated," according to the dispatch, and demanded to speak with the lead investigator on the case. After Enterkin received confirmation Tonya's father had been notified of her death, he returned Tim's call. Tim started the conversation by demanding all the information Enterkin had to that point, but Enterkin said he wouldn't discuss the case over the phone. He wanted Tim to come to the police station the next morning, and Tim said he'd try to be there but needed to make sure he found someone to take care of his son first.

Just past midnight on January 2, Davidson called the police again. This time he was frantic. He said a suspicious brown truck, possibly used in Tonya's murder, kept driving by his home. He said three people were in the truck, although he couldn't tell if they were male or female, because the windows were tinted.

The police told him to stay inside and call back in the morning.

2

DEVIL'S POINT

One day after his ex-girlfriend and the mother of his 18-month-old son was murdered, Tim Davidson showed up at the Pensacola Police Department for his first face-to-face interview.

He started by giving Enterkin the names of people he'd heard Tonya was out with on New Year's Eve — a collection of people he called "sluts, drug addicts and alcoholics" that included Tonya's cousin/best friend, Vanita Winchester, and Vanita's husband, Larry Winchester. Tim said he was best friends with Larry since he was 16 years old, but the two had recently had a falling-out. According to Tim, Tonya and Tim Jr. moved out of his home on December 27 and moved in with Vanita, Larry and their two young sons.

Enterkin already had some basic facts about Tonya in place by the time he spoke with Tim. He already knew Vanita, Larry and Tonya had all been out on New Year's Eve but parted ways shortly after midnight at Darryl's Bar & Grille, a popular nightclub and restaurant only a few miles from where Tonya's body was found.

Tim said the last time he'd seen Tonya was on New Year's Eve at the Cordova Mall, where she refused to speak with him. Tim suspected Tonya was in sexual relationships with two or maybe three other men at the time of her death. One of them was a male stripper who lived in Gulf Breeze, a small town just across the bay from Pensacola on the way to Pensacola Beach. Another man Tim named was Kurt Lisk, a part-time bartender/DJ at Darryl's, where Tonya was last seen on New Year's Eve. Tim said he was at a party with two women on New Year's Eve in Pace, a town about 20 minutes from Pensacola, and he'd been with one or both of them all night. Enterkin called both women, who confirmed Tim's alibi. In a rarity for the early 1980s, there was even a video recording of Tim at the party.

Enterkin went to Larry and Vanita's home to speak with them after he spoke with Tim. According to the couple, New Year's Eve started with the three of them at a house party hosted by Chris Grenier, one of Tonya and Vanita's classmates at Coastal Training Institute, which was a vocational school in Pensacola. At the party, they said Tonya drank a few glasses of wine, smoked a joint and ate a bowl of chili. From there, they went to Club 2001, where there was a $15 cover charge no one wanted to pay so they went to Darryl's. Vanita saw Tonya drink two strawberry daiquiris and a half bottle of champagne before she and Larry had to leave around 12:15 a.m. to pick up their two sons and Tonya's son from the babysitter. Before they parted ways, Vanita said she thought Tonya mentioned getting a ride home from some friends who were at the bar.

Vanita gave details about the physical abuse she'd seen Tonya suffer at Tim's hands. Once, in the parking lot at a Waffle House where Tonya worked, she saw him try to run her over with his truck. Another time, outside of Larry and Vanita's house, Tim tried to hit Tonya with his truck when she was pregnant. Tim didn't realize Larry was home, and when Larry saw what was happening, he came outside, dragged Tim out of his truck and "beat the ever-living shit out of him," according to Vanita. Larry only stopped when Tim curled up into the fetal position. Enterkin assumed this was the "falling-out" Tim referred to. Another time, Vanita said she was at Tim and Tonya's home and saw him slap Tonya. In response, Tonya picked up a cowboy boot, waited until Tim sat down on the couch then came up from behind and hit him in the side of the head with the heel of the boot, almost knocking him out.

"She wasn't someone you could just hit and get away with it," Vanita said. "She usually fought back."

Vanita said Tonya was in casual relationships with three men: the male stripper in Gulf Breeze, Lisk and a man in Pensacola named Robert Touchette. Tonya told Vanita she blew off Touchette on New Year's Eve because she hoped to meet up with Lisk. After speaking with Larry and Vanita, Enterkin went to Darryl's, where the bar's owners assembled almost everyone working on New Year's Eve with the notable exception of Lisk, who was left out at Enterkin's request. Four of Lisk's co-workers said they saw him at the bar talking with Tonya between 12:30 a.m. and 1:15 a.m., although none had any idea if the two were in a sexual relationship. No one saw them leave together, and several of the employees said after the bar closed, they'd partied together in the parking lot until almost dawn.

Enterkin took several officers with him to Lisk's home, and, after talking briefly, Lisk agreed to go with them back to the police station for an interview. Lisk said he talked to Tonya at the bar for the last time around 12:50 a.m. but left Darryl's with a different woman, Donita Pose. From the bar, he said they went to the home of a woman named Faye Chancey and were joined by Lisk's roommate, Jordan Bouknight. Lisk said he left Chancey's house for 15 to 20 minutes to get a bottle of wine but returned directly to the house and spent the night with Chancey while Bouknight and Pose left and spent the night together at Lisk's house.

Lisk denied ever having a sexual relationship with Tonya and agreed to take a polygraph test, which he passed.

That night, Tonya's purse was brought to the police station by a person who found it around 11 a.m. on New Year's Day — approximately one mile from where her body was found — then saw a report about the murder on the evening news. The purse still contained Tonya's driver's license and everything else she stored in it.

※ ※ ※

Tonya's murder was the main story on the front page of the *Pensacola News Journal* on Wednesday, January 2, accompanied by a photo of Bob Grant and Assistant Crime Scene Supervisor Teresa Williams standing under an umbrella on Peacock Drive and looking at Tonya's body underneath a large white tarp. Enterkin told the newspaper he suspected Tonya was brought to Peacock Drive from somewhere else, which was where the crime likely occurred. The newspaper also talked to Mary Lloyd and someone identified only as an "elderly man" who lived on Peacock Drive — presumably John Laabs — who asked his name not be used in the article.

"We have a lot of excitement in Devil's Point," the elderly man said, referencing the nickname for the sprawling neighborhood around the bluffs. "The train derailment, the plane crash in the bay ... and now a dead body."

✿ ✿ ✿

On the evening of November 9, 1977, two freight train cars from the Louisville & Nashville Company carrying toxic anhydrous ammonia, a liquefied gas, crashed on the train tracks directly below the bluffs at Escambia Bay. The gas fumes from the punctured freight train cars shot up and over the bluffs and directly into the yard where Dr. Jon Thorsov and his wife, Lloyda, were eating dinner outside with their four-year-old daughter and one-year-old son. Immediately realizing the danger they were in, Dr. Thorsov and his wife covered their children's faces and managed to make it inside their home as the fumes caught up with them. Still spilling out of the punctured freight train cars at a terrifying rate, the gas began to move toward Peacock Drive until, at the last second, a gigantic gust of wind blew it back the other way, out past the bluffs and out over the water. This single gust of wind — this act of nature — prevented what would have been one of the deadliest manmade disasters in American history. It just didn't come soon enough to save the Thorsovs.

Dr. Thorsov died within minutes of the gas coming over the bluffs. His wife died several weeks later. The children survived thanks to the quick thinking of their parents but were hospitalized for months following the crash. Both children required years of full-time medical care and, represented by famed Pensacola attorney Fred Levin, were paid $18 million in a settlement from the L&N Company as part of the $50 million total paid out to 46 victims of the crash.

On May 8, 1978 — six months after the train crash — National Airlines Flight 193 was traveling nonstop from Miami to Pensacola when it crash-landed into the water in Escambia Bay and just offshore from the bluffs and the railroad tracks. The Boeing 727 airplane sank in 12 feet of water, and three of the passengers died by drowning after they mistook their seats for flotation devices.

The National Transportation Safety Board placed the blame for the crash squarely on the shoulders of the flight crew. The official report from the NTSB found several catastrophic mistakes led to the crash, including trying an approach to land on a runway both the pilot and co-pilot were told was closed before taking off from Miami. The pilots also misread the plane's altimeter and thought they were coming out of a bank of fog at an elevation of 1,500 feet. They discovered instead they were just 500 feet over Escambia Bay and were forced to crash the plane into the water.

3

OUR DARLING

Tonya's family buried her in a long, white dress with a collar large enough to cover up the bruises on her neck from where she'd been strangled to death. It was an open-casket funeral, which surprised many of those in attendance.

"There she was, this gorgeous girl, and she looked awful," said Deb Adkins, Tonya's cousin and Vanita's older sister. "She'd been strangled and beaten and was all swollen up and puffy. I remember how sad the whole thing was. The first days of the year are always supposed to be this really hopeful time, and that was the way our family started off that year, with her murder hanging over all of our heads. And as if that wasn't bad enough ... we all had to show up and see what someone had done to her."

Outside the funeral home, undercover police officers took pictures of the attendees and their cars as they showed up. Enterkin set up a hidden camera at the lectern, facing out at the audience to take pictures of everyone in their seats. Tonya's parents sat in the front row with her older sister, Renee, who sat next to Vanita and Larry. Tim sat on the other side of the chapel, surrounded by friends and family.

After the funeral, Renee asked Tim where Tim Jr. was and when she and her parents could see him again, but he ignored her, refusing to even make eye contact. Davidson later told Vanita he'd left Tim Jr. with his sister.

Tonya was buried in the family plot at Crain Cemetery in Milton. Her family ordered a heart-shaped, marble headstone with a picture of Tonya holding Tim Jr. embossed on the front.

Below the picture and above Tonya's name, two words were carved into the marble: *Our Darling.*

❖ ❖ ❖

After the funeral, Enterkin interviewed Vanita for a second time. This time, without her husband there, she gave more details about the week leading up to Tonya's murder. She said Tonya and Tim Jr. moved in with them just a few days after Christmas, following another fight with Tim. It wasn't the first time Tonya came to stay with them, but Vanita noticed something different this time.

"She brought her stuff with her ... like all of her stuff," Vanita said. "She'd never done that before. A few days after she moved in, she asked me to drive her and Tim Jr. out to Milton to see our families, so we went on the day before New Year's Eve. That night, after we got home (from Milton) ... we went out and got a little wasted."

The night of December 30, after returning home from seeing family, Vanita and Tonya went to a dive bar called Richey's in Pensacola and at some point, during an evening of heavy drinking, Tonya left with a man she'd met at the bar. Vanita said she waited in the bar's parking lot in her car for several hours until Tonya returned. Vanita was furious because she knew the friction it would cause with her husband for coming home so late. The next day, nursing massive hangovers, Tonya and Vanita went to the mall to shop for New Year's Eve outfits, where Tim showed up and Tonya ignored him. After he left, Tonya told Vanita she wanted to meet up with Lisk or the man she'd left the bar with the previous night, who told her he'd try to blow off his date and meet up with her if he could.

Enterkin finished the day confirming Lisk's alibi that he'd been with his roommate, Jordan Bouknight, and two women, Faye Chancey and Donita Pose, from when he'd left Darryl's shortly before 2 a.m. until the next morning except for a 15- to 20-minute trip home to get a bottle of wine. Bouknight said he saw Tonya and Lisk talking at the bar at Darryl's just before 1 a.m. and then saw Lisk leave the bar with Donita Pose. He'd seen Tonya at the bar by herself and looking "preoccupied" close to 2 a.m. Bouknight said he met Lisk, Pose and Chancey at Chancey's house after he left work, and the only time he saw Lisk leave was when he went to get wine from their house and bring it back home. Bouknight left Lisk and Pose at Chancey's house and took Chancey back to the house he shared with Lisk, where they spent the night together. It was the same story, almost to a word, that Lisk, Pose and Chancey had already told to the police.

Enterkin gave a frank assessment of his investigation in an article that ran in the Saturday, January 5, edition of the *Pensacola News Journal*: "We have no motive, no reason, no suspect," Enterkin said. "She'd been strangled with some object other than a hand. She'd been dead only a short time. We've narrowed down the time (of death) between 2 a.m. and 5 a.m. on New Year's Day. We're trying to trace her movements during this time. We'd also like all the help we can get from anybody who knew this woman."

4

TONYA

Growing up, Renee Ethridge found the roles between herself and her younger sister flip-flopped, which meant even though Tonya was four years younger, she was the one making the decisions for both of them. More often than not, that led to both of them landing in some sort of trouble with their parents. While Tonya was full of mischief and carried herself like she was bulletproof, Renee made her way in the world by keeping quiet, which was mainly to avoid her father's wrath. Joe Ethridge doted on Tonya but always seemed to regard his older daughter with disdain. When their father focused his rage on Renee, she wore it like a badge of honor.

"I told myself ... at least he's not doing this to Tonya," Renee said. "And that got me through it."

By the time Tonya was in middle school, she was waking Renee up in the middle of the night to sneak out and meet boys at a park down the street from their home. Two of those boys, Larry and Michael McKinley, were brothers who ended up marrying the two sisters. Renee married Larry, the older of the brothers, not long after she graduated from Milton High School in 1976. Tonya dropped out of high school her sophomore year and married Michael in 1978, when she was 17 years old and he was 19 years old. At that time, Florida law allowed minors who were 16 or 17 years old to get married as long as the other person wasn't more than two years older.

Michael and Tonya lived with his family in the Tampa area for the first year of their marriage before moving back to Pensacola. Michael took to married life right away and seemed to have genuine love and affection for his young wife. Tonya, like a lot of 18-year-olds, wanted to party. It would spell disaster for their marriage.

❈ ❈ ❈

Vanita married Larry Winchester around the same time Tonya and Michael moved into a duplex in Pensacola next door to Tim Davidson's older brother, Kelvin Davidson.

Tim and Larry met when they were teenagers, when Larry was riding his motorcycle down an alley behind Tim's aunt's house on his way to pick Vanita up for a date. Tim was standing in the alley and asked Larry the most stoner question of all time as he rode by — "Got papers?" — and the two rolled up a joint, smoked it together and a friendship was born. This was in 1975 or 1976, depending on who you asked.

Not long after Tonya and Michael moved into the duplex, Tonya began having an affair with Tim that seemed to arise almost out of convenience. Most days, Kelvin and Michael were at work while Tim and Tonya, both jobless, stayed home. The affair only came to light after Tim and Tonya were involved in a car crash that put them both in the hospital. Even after that, Michael was still willing to take Tonya back. She chose Tim instead.

"Tonya was very sweet, very kind," Kelvin said. "So it always surprised me she would want to be with Tim and that Vanita was her best friend because they were both incredibly selfish, vindictive people."

Tim and Tonya's relationship seemed to have two constants: They were always fighting, and they were always broke. Sometimes Tim worked and they had a place to live. Other times they lived with Kelvin or wherever they knew there was an open room. Tim was controlling and jealous to the point that a casual conversation between Tonya and another man would send him into a rage, so he limited her contact with her immediate family and close friends, aside from

Vanita and her father. Tonya was known as a person who didn't like to be bossed around, so her being in a relationship with someone so controlling caught her family and friends by surprise. The alcohol and drugs omnipresent during their relationship only made things more volatile, and when their fights got physical, the police were rarely called. When the cops did show up, Tim could almost always talk his way out of it. The pattern between Tim and Tonya became very predictable. Blowout fight. Tonya moves out. Tim shows up somewhere begging to get her back. Tonya folds and takes him back.

As the relationship spiraled out of control, Tonya hit a low point when she was arrested for marijuana possession in November 1981 as part of a sting at a home in Gulf Breeze, which resulted in five people being arrested. Four years later, the fingerprints from the arrest were used to identify Tonya's body.

✿ ✿ ✿

Toward the end of 1982, Tonya discovered she was pregnant. She told Vanita there were three men she believed could be the father, including Tim Davidson and Michael McKinley, who she was still legally married to but had been separated from for several years. The third man, who Tonya said she thought was most likely the father, told her he wanted nothing to do with the child.

Vanita accompanied Tonya when she went to tell Tim about the pregnancy, where she insisted it was his child. After an initial fight over the child's paternity, the two reconciled and Tim began to proudly tell friends and family he was going to be a father.

On July 26, 1983, Tonya gave birth to a boy, Timothy Harley Davidson Jr. "Tim and Tonya Davidson" were listed as the parents in the birth announcement in the newspaper. It's the only time Tonya's last name is ever listed as Davidson in any sort of public record.

✿ ✿ ✿

Tonya's marriage to Michael McKinley officially came to an end on June 27, 1984. On paper, they were married for six years but only lived together as husband and wife for a little over two years.

In the fall of 1984, Tonya and Vanita enrolled at the Coastal Training Institute to take a one-year course in secretarial work. It was Tonya's first attempt at formal education since she'd dropped out of high school in the tenth grade.

Unsurprisingly, having a child together did not make Tim and Tonya's relationship stronger. Instead, the frequency and veracity of their fights increased, as did the times Tonya and Tim Jr. showed up at Larry and Vanita's house to get away from Tim. As all of this was happening, Tonya became imbued with a new sense of confidence, thanks in large part to the classes she was taking and the idea she could create a life for herself and Tim Jr. on her own. By the end of her first semester at CTI, Tonya decided it was time to end things with Tim for good, and for the first time in her life, she began to plan a future that didn't revolve around a man she was in a relationship with.

❖ ❖ ❖

The day Vanita drove Tonya and Tim Jr. to Milton to see their family — December 30, 1984 — was the first time Renee had a chance to be alone with her younger sister in several years and the last time she would see her alive. The relationship between Tim and Renee was particularly volatile and had transitioned from intense dislike to open animosity after Renee found out Tim was physically abusing Tonya. Meek by nature, Renee seemed to flip a switch when she saw Tim. These were two people, for the most part, who could not be in the same room together for any amount of time without shit starting to pop off.

"Too much had happened between them that we knew about," Renee said. "[Tim] tried to hit Tonya with his truck, twice. He beat her up. He threw her out in the rain, barefoot, when she was pregnant, and our dad had to go pick her up that time. So, the day she came to see us, I got her alone and just asked over and over 'What's wrong? What's wrong?' And every time she just shook her head. She wouldn't say what it was. She just told me that she loved me and that she just really wanted to see everyone. To me, looking back, it was like she was trying to say goodbye."

Renee had a short telephone conversation with Tonya and Vanita the day after the visit as they were at Vanita's house getting ready to go out on New Year's Eve; then she couldn't reach Tonya on New Year's Day. Later that day, several of Renee's cousins showed up at her home to tell her Tonya was dead. Renee's mother, Laverne, didn't have a phone at the time, so Renee left her home and went directly to her mother so she could be the one to tell her what happened.

Vanita said someone called and told her Tonya was dead, but she hung up on them, thinking it was a sick joke. More calls, in rapid succession, convinced her it was real. Renee and her father drove to Pensacola to identify Tonya's body in the morgue, but neither could bring themselves to do it. Instead, Vanita and one of Tonya's aunts agreed to identify the body. Inside the morgue, they went into a room where Tonya's body was on a cold steel table and covered almost entirely by a white sheet. Vanita was shown her face and her hand with the "M" tattoos on the knuckles to make a positive ID.

"It seemed like she was dirty ... like she'd been in the actual dirt, which it turned out she had been," Vanita said. "That was striking to me because she'd been dressed up so nice to go out."

Later that night, Tonya's father called Vanita and lashed out, screaming at her over the phone. He wasn't the only one in the family who blamed Vanita for Tonya's death. For Vanita, the guilt was overwhelming. It never went away.

"He kept screaming at me, saying, 'You wouldn't leave a dog like you left my daughter at the bar,' over and over," Vanita said. "Somehow, that's what they always believed. That it was my fault."

5

FUMBLE

No single person did more to set back Tonya's murder investigation in its early stages than Pensacola Police Department Crime Scene Supervisor Bob Grant.

Grant was second on the scene at Peacock Drive after patrol officer Ken Franks arrived sometime after 3 a.m. on New Year's Day, and it was Grant who made the snap decision on Tonya's cause of death. His theory, after spending just a few minutes with Tonya's body, was that Mary Lloyd or her daughter, Sharon Edwards, killed Tonya by running her over with their vehicle on the way to take their dog to an all-night veterinary clinic. Grant told them as much when he said they weren't allowed to leave their home to take their sick dog to a vet clinic.

"[Grant] said her hips were broken and they'd gone and done measurements on our tires and that we'd hit her with our car," Mary said, "which was just ridiculous. It seemed obvious someone just pulled up and dumped her where she was by how her body was placed."

Within an hour, a different set of cops — not Grant or Franks — knocked on Mary's door and told her Tonya hadn't been run over by a car and they were free to leave. By then, the sun was starting to come up, and the street was filling up with people who were curious about what was going on. Fearful of causing more commotion and having to answer more questions from their neighbors, Mary and her family decided to stay home.

On the official report filed by Franks, he stated his work on the case didn't begin until 5 a.m. despite Lloyd, her daughter and her daughter's boyfriend all saying they called the police sometime after 3 a.m. and Franks was there within minutes. Franks also makes no mention of Grant's initial theory about Tonya's death in his report. The approximately two- to three-hour time gap between when the three witnesses who found the body said the police arrived and when the official report says the investigation began has never been accounted for.

And it was in those few, precious hours early in the investigation that the killer had remained close by, unabated and lurking in the shadows and free to cover his tracks.

6

CASEFILE 1985

As the Pensacola Police Department's authority on forensics, Grant had the final say on the cause of death in Tonya's case. Shamed out of his first theory of Mary Lloyd's van being involved in a hit-and-run killing, Grant nailed the layup on Tonya's actual cause of death, which went in his report as "strangulation with a thin object" and seemed largely derived from Enterkin's work at the crime scene.

From there, Grant went off the rails. The small, blue towel left by Tonya's head was found to contain semen, male pubic hair, male head hair and black dog hair. Semen was also found in Tonya's vagina and anus, along with black dog hair on her clothes and body. While Grant didn't have the advantage of DNA testing in 1985, it would be just making excuses to call his early work anything but grossly incompetent. The wealth of evidence, along with injuries to Tonya's body and how her body was left — breasts exposed, pantyhose ripped and pulled down around her ankle — seemed to indicate with a high level of certainty she'd been a victim of sexual assault. Enterkin and Assistant Crime Scene Analyst Carolynn Stephens both agreed on this point. Grant did not.

In his final report, Grant went a step further. He wrote there was no evidence of sexual assault or even sexual activity, and no one could officially overrule him. His conclusion, however bewildering as it may have been, would serve as the final word on the case.

When Tonya's family asked, they were definitively told there was no evidence she'd been raped.

❖ ❖ ❖

The day after Tonya's funeral, Tim went to the police station and passed a polygraph test. Because he also had a solid alibi for the night of the crime, Enterkin was able to rule out the one person who would ostensibly be the prime suspect in a case like this: the estranged husband/lover/boyfriend/baby daddy.

Enterkin spent the days after the funeral clearing more suspects. He chased down a rumor that two men Tim worked with, George Close and Hershell Grant, raped and murdered Tonya. Close and Grant said they were together at several parties on New Year's Eve until 4 a.m. and then passed out at a friend's house, which was confirmed by the friend. Close, Grant and the friend they stayed with all came in and passed polygraph tests.

Robert Pollard also passed a polygraph test. He had lived with Tonya and Tim for about a month before Tonya moved out. Enterkin went to the Coastal Training Institute and interviewed Chris Grenier, the classmate identified as the host of the New Year's Eve party attended by Tonya, Vanita and Larry. Grenier confirmed Tonya was at the party until around 10:30 p.m. and saw her smoke pot and drink two glasses of wine while she was there.

At the request of Enterkin and Stephens, Pensacola police chief Louis Goss reached out to the FBI Laboratory Unit on January 7, 1985, asking for help with forensic microanalysis work in Tonya's case. Goss' letter to the FBI gave the basic details of the case with an emphasis on the need for analysis of the samples of male pubic hair and male head hair. Within a week, the FBI responded and let the Pensacola police know they could help them with whatever they needed moving forward.

Stephens immediately sent a large amount of physical evidence to the FBI to analyze, with the request it be returned to Pensacola afterward. This included the blue towel found beside Tonya's body; her dress and pantyhose; nail scrapings from her hands; fibers removed from Tonya's mouth, back and legs; plus jewelry, shoes, the blood sample kit and a sexual assault kit. Stephens also sent along all of the forensic evidence collected from the few suspects they'd already identified, including blood and saliva samples.

On January 8, Enterkin interviewed Gary and Michelle Simmons, the couple Vanita said she saw Tonya talking with when she left Tonya at Darryl's Bar & Grille. They told Enterkin they saw Tonya talking to a man named Chris Grenier when they left and also described a tall, thin, blond man in his early 20s who'd been sitting at the bar and who the people in their group thought was acting "suspicious." They said he had a thin nose, wore gold-framed glasses and had a dark suit on. Enterkin confirmed Chris Grenier stayed out with friends until 4 a.m., and another man, John Rahn — who Tonya's friends said paid her bar tab on a previous trip to Darryl's — had a solid alibi, went into the police station and passed a polygraph test. Enterkin wasn't able to track down the tall, thin, blond man at the bar who Tonya's friends said was acting suspiciously.

On January 17, Vanita called Enterkin to tell him she remembered that the man Tonya left a bar in Pensacola with on the night before New Year's Eve was named James, and when Enterkin went to the bar with Vanita's description of the man, he learned his full name was James Holt. At the address listed on Holt's driver's license, Holt's mother said he and his wife unexpectedly moved to Houma, Louisiana, on January 2, after he found work on an offshore oil rig.

Enterkin contacted Holt's wife the next day. She said on New Year's Eve they went to a bar in Pensacola and returned home by 11 p.m. and that she fell asleep before midnight watching TV. To her knowledge, her husband didn't leave the house again. Holt got word on the oil rig that the police were looking to talk with him and called Enterkin to say he was going to return home two days ahead of schedule to meet in person. When Holt went into the station, he willingly gave hair and blood samples, allowed police to search his car and agreed to take a polygraph test, which he passed. Holt and his wife divorced in 1991.

At the request of the FBI, Enterkin tracked down the manufacturer of the blue towel found by Tonya's head and discovered it was only sold at one store in Pensacola, but that didn't amount to much. Toward the end of January, Enterkin began to feel like he was hitting a wall in his investigation, but at the beginning of February, things began to pick back up after Enterkin received an updated list from Darryl's of the employees who were working on New Year's Eve. This new list included names that weren't on the initial list.

On February 11, Stephens received the FBI's forensics report on the evidence she had sent them in January, along with the evidence returned to Pensacola. The FBI report established that in all likelihood the male head hair, pubic hair and semen came from the same person. The semen was found in three different places — in Tonya's vagina, anus and the towel left by her body — and was all from someone with type A blood. The pubic hair and head hair were from a white male with brown or sandy blond hair color. The dog hair was all black and likely to have come from one animal.

Faced with the FBI report confirming the presence of semen and pubic hair and that it was all likely from the same person, Grant continued to insist there was no evidence of sexual assault or even sexual activity before Tonya's death. Enterkin voiced his dissent in the most straightforward way possible but this time made sure it ended up in the official record.

"Bob Grant has informed that there was no evidence of intercourse found in the autopsy," Enterkin wrote. "From the way the body was dressed at the time she was found and the presence of pubic hair on the towel, it appears to me that she did have sex prior to death."

⁂

Jeffrey Brunt wasn't on the initial list given to Enterkin of employees working at Darryl's on New Year's Eve because New Year's Eve was his first day of working there. When Darryl's management gave Enterkin an updated list in March 1985, Brunt's name was on it, and Enterkin went to his house to talk with him.

Brunt said he washed dishes in the kitchen until approximately 1 a.m., and after his shift ended, he only had $2 on him so he bought one beer, drank it and walked home because his car wasn't working. He said both of his parents were asleep when he returned home, and while he said he didn't know Tonya, he knew the neighborhood her body was dumped in because he'd lived there before. He also said he'd heard rumors it was a drug-related killing.

Two things caught Enterkin's attention right away. Brunt had light brown hair and owned several dogs with black hair, which matched the FBI forensics report. Enterkin asked Brunt if he'd be willing to come in and take a polygraph test.

"Polygraph test is only as good as the person giving it," Brunt said. "But I'll do it."

Brunt called Enterkin the day he was scheduled to come in to say he was no longer willing to take the polygraph after speaking with an attorney. This was probably sound legal advice because within a decade, polygraph tests were considered inadmissible in almost every court in the U.S.

Enterkin asked Brunt to come in just to talk and he agreed, as long as they were clear he wasn't going to do the polygraph. This time, parts of Brunt's story began to change. Where he initially said both of his parents were asleep when he returned home, he now said his father was awake and watching "The Tonight Show." Enterkin asked Brunt if he would consider taking the polygraph test and, despite the advice from his attorney, Brunt agreed. As the test went along, Brunt became more and more hostile to the questioning, and about halfway through he removed the equipment attached to his body and said he was leaving.

"You've got more than you need," Brunt said as he walked out.

Enterkin moved Brunt's name to the top of the suspect list. A few days after the interrupted polygraph examination, Enterkin went to Brunt's house while he was at work and asked his mother for permission to have a forensics team collect animal hair and any other possible evidence from inside the home, but she refused. Enterkin obtained a search warrant for samples of Brunt's head hair and pubic hair, along with hair samples from his dogs. Stephens immediately sent the new evidence to the FBI lab and asked for comparisons to the head hair, pubic hair and animal hair samples found at the crime scene.

* * *

On March 1, exactly two months after Tonya's body was found, 29-year-old Patricia Stephens was killed in Pensacola in a manner that bore several striking resemblances to Tonya's murder. Patricia was raped, beaten and strangled to death before her body was dumped just a few miles west of Tonya's body, on Saufley Pines Road. Just like Tonya, she was dumped on the side of the road, and just like Tonya, she was left half-naked, with her breasts and genitals exposed. Both women had similar lifestyles that were considered morally "dangerous" by police standards — whatever that meant — because Tonya was arrested for drugs in 1981, while Patricia was arrested for drugs in 1975 and for prostitution in 1984.

Despite Enterkin already running an investigation that could have presumably folded the new case into the one he was already working on, the Escambia County Sheriff's Office took the case. It was a jurisdictional quirk that Pensacola police and the ECSO worked crimes in the same areas around the edges of Pensacola — like where Patricia's body was found — and when that happened, the case sometimes went to whoever showed up first.

❖ ❖ ❖

A few days after Patricia's body was found, a pair of anonymous calls were placed to local television station WEAR-TV and the *Pensacola News Journal* by a man who identified himself as the "Pensacola Strangler" and claimed responsibility for both murders. He claimed there was an additional, third body buried behind the Escambia County Jail, and once police located that third body he would advise authorities on where a fourth body could be found.

In the call to WEAR-TV, the man also recited a poem:

I'm the Pensacola Strangler
Beware of me
For you'll never know,
Who the next victim will be
I love to choke young lady's [sic] necks
And make the police a nervous wreck

Pensacola authorities dismissed the caller's claims of being a serial killer when no bodies were found buried behind the Escambia County Jail, although how they were able to determine this wasn't disclosed in the newspaper.

Through the summer and fall, the pace of Enterkin's investigation continued to slow. On October 14, in a memo to his bosses, Enterkin disclosed he'd run out of leads and suspects.

"I recommend this case be inactivated until such a time as a definite suspect is identified," Enterkin wrote.

7

WEB OF LIES

When Pensacola police investigator Ted Chamberlain heard Tonya's case was going to be declared inactive, he convinced Enterkin to take another look at a suspect Chamberlain thought slipped through the cracks early on.

When Kurt Lisk passed his polygraph test in January, Chamberlain openly expressed discomfort about clearing him as a suspect but couldn't properly articulate what he felt was "off" until he went back over the results from the polygraph test. The notes on the case indicated Lisk sat for an extensive, three-hour interview with the police right before the polygraph was administered, which was a huge no-no when it came to polygraphy tests, because that length of questioning could skew the results. Chamberlain also pointed out that the questions from the test and the interview were similar enough that Lisk's answers shouldn't have been considered valid, and neither should the results that said he'd passed.

"[Chamberlain] felt we'd been misled by the initial results," Enterkin wrote in his report.

Enterkin and Chamberlain went to Lisk's home to tell him they were starting the investigation over from scratch and wanted him to take another polygraph test, but this time they wanted to do it without the interview beforehand. Lisk agreed to take the test again and came to the station a few days later. This time, he failed miserably.

Enterkin immediately began tracking down the three people Lisk used as his alibi on New Year's Eve — Jordan Bouknight, Donita Pose and Faye Chancey. In January, all three told the police they were with Lisk for all but 15-20 minutes from around 1:30 a.m. until the next morning, with Chancey and Lisk spending the night together. Enterkin went after Pose first. Right away, she admitted she lied in January. The truth, she said, was Lisk didn't show up at Chancey's house until sometime past 2:30 a.m. and she lied about his whereabouts because Chancey asked her to do so. Enterkin had officers track down Chancey and Bouknight and bring them to the station. Chancey admitted she lied without much prompting. Bouknight admitted to lying before Enterkin even had a chance to sit down in the interview room.

"I gave a false statement in January," Bouknight said. "I'm admitting it."

By 6:30 p.m., Lisk was back at the station sitting across from Enterkin and Chamberlain.

٭ ٭ ٭

Enterkin and Chamberlain began by questioning Lisk about where he was on New Year's Eve and into the early morning hours of New Year's Day. Lisk just shook his head.

"Did you tell me the truth about what you know about Tonya's murder?" Enterkin asked.

"You wouldn't believe me if I told you," Lisk said.

Enterkin and Chamberlain both sat in stunned silence.

Lisk said he couldn't remember if Tonya had ever been in his car. He continued to deny ever having sex with her and said he couldn't remember his blood type. Less than an hour into the interview, Lisk's father showed up, told the police his son wasn't answering any more questions and took him home. Lisk agreed to return to the police station several days later to give hair and blood samples but didn't show up and didn't return calls. Within a few days, Enterkin was informed through a third party that Lisk now had an attorney. Chancey was scheduled to come in for another interview and didn't show up. A few hours later, Lisk called Enterkin to tell him she wasn't coming in because she needed to speak with an attorney first.

In response, Enterkin obtained a search warrant for Lisk's 1965 Mustang and had the car impounded and combed over for physical evidence that was then sent to the FBI lab.

Bouknight returned to the police station and gave sworn testimony to Assistant State Attorney David Rimmer, under oath, that Lisk told him on multiple occasions before New Year's Eve that he'd had sex with Tonya.

8

QUANTICO

The Pensacola Police Department gained an important ally early in the investigation with the FBI, and the person most responsible for nurturing that relationship was Assistant Crime Scene Analyst Carolynn Stephens, who had only been on the job for six months before she was called to Peacock Drive on New Year's Day to fill in for a co-worker.

Stephens' career in law enforcement was a case study in determination. After finishing first in her police academy class at Pensacola State College, Stephens was told by Police Chief Louis Goss that at just 5 feet and 100 pounds, she was too small to be an officer. It was heartbreaking news for Stephens, who had wanted to be a cop for as long as she could remember.

Stephens went to work full-time for a doctor's office in Pensacola but kept a part-time job with the PPD's police auxiliary unit, which was run by Crime Scene Supervisor Bob Grant, who was also one of her professors at the police academy. After a few months, Grant approached Stephens about working for him on the police department's forensics team as a crime scene analyst. Since she'd already made it through the police academy with flying colors, he told her if she could pass the written test for forensics she would have a job.

The test required Stephens to look at photos and evidence slides from a crime scene and then write up reports and answer a series of questions based on what she saw. When Stephens went to take the test, she realized it was the same one Grant used for one of his classes at the academy. She aced the test, again, got the job and worked for the Pensacola police for 26 years until her retirement in 2010.

At the time of Tonya's murder, Stephens lived just a few blocks from Peacock Drive and was called to fill in on the morning of New Year's Day despite it being her day off. From the start, Stephens liked her work to be meticulous.

"I would even get mad if it seemed like my handwriting (in the report) didn't look exactly the same every single time," Stephens said. "I know people would get frustrated with me, but when I got called into court to testify ... it was really easy to point to what I did without any uncertainty."

In her dealings with the FBI, Stephens displayed an advanced understanding of modern forensics and professionalism that won over her counterparts in Quantico. So much so that the FBI decided to lend use of its most valuable weapon in solving crimes to the PPD for Tonya's case in the form of the brilliant minds at the Behavioral Science Unit (BSU), National Center for the Analysis of Violent Crime (NCAVC) and the FBI Academy. It was the same group of people who would eventually become the basis for bestselling novels, movies and TV shows like "The Silence of the Lambs" and David Fincher's Netflix series "Mindhunter," based on the nonfiction book by former FBI agent John Douglas and Mark Olshaker.

James Cagnassola Jr. was in charge of the FBI field office in Jacksonville at the time and commissioned an extensive criminal psychological profile for Tonya's case from FBI profiler William H. Hagerty Jr.

Hagerty's profile included four sections: Victimology, Analysis of the Medical Examiner's Report, Crime Scene Assessment and Offender Profile. After the profile was reviewed by both the Behavioral Science Unit and the FBI Academy, it was sent to Pensacola.

"This criminal profile contains information of a confidential and sensitive nature," Hagerty wrote in his introduction. "It is provided exclusively for your investigative assistance and should not be

disseminated except to other criminal justice agencies with a legiti-
mate investigative or prosecutorial interest in this matter."

The Victimology section of the profile focused on Tonya's lifestyle
and how vulnerable she was on the night of her murder.

"The victim is a 23-year-old white female; she was not a prostitute
but was known to be sexually promiscuous," Hagerty wrote. "She also
liked to party ... and had a great love for marijuana."

Tests showed Tonya's system had high levels of marijuana in it
when she died, and Hagerty drew a line between her murder and her
drug arrest in 1981.

"Victim is described as a 'fighter' who was very headstrong and
preferred older men, but had been living with a long-haired 'hippy'
type for some time," Hagerty wrote, presumably talking about Tim
Davidson, who had long, red hair at the time. "She was known to walk
or hitchhike to get where she wanted to go and appeared to be very
confident and able to handle any situation. She would apparently go
with almost anyone if he promised her marijuana. McKinley is what
we consider a 'high risk' victim as a result of her lifestyle, including
her promiscuity and love for marijuana. She might have been considered a 'fighter,' but this does not really affect the fact that her loose
lifestyle made her extremely likely to be a victim of a violent crime
such as this. It is very difficult ... to determine whether she was a victim of opportunity or specifically selected. However, it would appear
that she was more of a victim of opportunity and that the attack on her
was in all likelihood spontaneous. It could either have been someone
that she met while waiting at Darryl's after her friends left or she
could have started home hitchhiking and was picked up by the even-
tual perpetrator of this crime."

By the end of the 1980s, the dangers of hitchhiking were largely
known and communicated to most of American society. In 1984,
those dangers were not as clear. How society viewed smoking marijuana was much different as well — California was still 12 years away
from becoming the first state to make marijuana legal for medical use.

"[Hagerty] said smoking marijuana and having sex made [Tonya]
high risk, which I thought was demeaning and too general," Stephens
said. "I mean, marijuana and sex are what got her killed? Really? I

wanted more than that from him. Now the part about hitchhiking? Hell yes, that mattered."

Leaving Tonya's body somewhere she could easily be found indicated to Hagerty there was no emotional attachment between victim and perpetrator. The brutal specifics of the medical examiner's report seemed to fall in line with Enterkin's initial assessment of the crime scene.

"The medical examiner determined that the cause of death was strangulation," Hagerty wrote. "This was based on fractures of the left side of the hyoid bone and some hemorrhage in the laryngeal muscles and epiglottis. There was a band-like, faint mark in the upper neck area which appears in one of the photographs. It measured 2 centimeters in width. This indicated that some type of belt or ligature was used to effect the strangulation, as opposed to manual strangulation. There was a large linear laceration on the back top portion of the head and a bruise on the right upper front region of the head. This appeared to be the result of an assault by a blunt instrument. There was no skull fracture and no significant injury to the underlying brain tissue, but blows of this magnitude, according to the medical examiner, could cause a concussion, which might render the victim unconscious or at least semiconscious. There are also some bruises and abrasions on the right hand and arm, which could have been defense wounds. Most of the other abrasions appear to have been caused by the victim being pulled over some rough surface or thrown onto a rough surface. There were also some scrape marks on her legs and her one arm."

While Hagerty wasn't dumb enough to assert Tonya didn't have sex that night, like Grant had, he chose an alternative not far above slut-shaming.

"In view of her promiscuity, it is not known whether the semen found in the vagina is the result of a sexual attack which occurred at this time or from a previous sexual activity," Hagerty wrote.

New Year's Eve added a new, confusing dimension to the investigation, which worked to the killer's advantage. Most of the time, no one was going to think twice about two people leaving a bar together. On New Year's Eve, that awareness would be even lower. It added to Hagerty's theory the crime was committed in the spur of the moment.

"Because the crime took place during the time many people consume alcohol to celebrate the New Year and because of the victim's reputation of association with drug users, it can be assumed the offender was very possibly under the influence of drugs and/or alcohol," Hagerty wrote. "The subject's use of either substance may have resulted in the disorganization observed. However, on the following day, he may have very well returned to a very organized type of lifestyle.

"The belief that he was not well organized is also substantiated by the fact that the weapons utilized by him in his efforts to control the victim were not a knife or a gun, which one would use if this was well planned in advance, but merely some type of blunt instrument and a belt or rope of some kind. It is definitely believed that the weapons used were ones of opportunity that just happened to be near at the time the offense occurred."

For the killer, this probably meant acting out a long-simmering sexual fantasy.

"He'd lived with the [fantasy] for some time but never had the opportunity before that night to bring it to reality," Hagerty wrote. "When he came upon this victim, it was probably a spontaneous move on his part to make sexual advances to her, and when she refused he lost control of himself, resulting in the confrontation, which led to his assaulting her with the blunt instrument that was available."

Just like Enterkin, Hagerty believed Tonya was taken from Darryl's to where the attack occurred and that it was somewhere private and close to where the body was found. Hagerty believed Tonya was lured with the promise of a ride, drugs or alcohol — possibly all three. Hagerty theorized the killer hit Tonya with a blunt object, dragged her somewhere he could sexually assault her and partially stripped her clothes off in the process of raping her. Then he strangled her to death before driving her body a short distance to Peacock Drive and dumping her in the empty lot. As he was driving away, the killer realized her shoes and purse were still in the car and threw them out the window. The fact the killer left behind so much physical evidence, specifically the towel with his semen and pubic hair in it, bolstered the "disorganized homicide" theory.

In the Offender Profile section of the report, Hagerty maintained the killer and Tonya were likely strangers. Tonya lacked injuries to her face, which were typically more severe when the killer was familiar with the victim. Tonya's injuries also led Hagerty to believe there was only a single perpetrator. Had there been multiple perpetrators, Hagerty did not believe Tonya could have resisted to the extent she did or would have sustained the injuries she did. Where the shoes and purse were discarded on specific, connecting side streets adjacent to Peacock Drive led Hagerty to believe the killer had intimate knowledge of the neighborhood in which the body was dumped.

"In all probability, the individual who committed the crime probably lives within a mile or two of where the shoes were located," Hagerty wrote.

9

PRIME SUSPECT

Kurt Lisk made himself the prime suspect in Tonya's murder after police uncovered a web of lies told by Lisk and his friends in the early days of the investigation. That the lies were told to conceal Lisk's whereabouts on the night of the murder and conceal a sexual relationship between Lisk and Tonya only deepened suspicions he was the killer.

While the lies were detrimental to the investigation, Enterkin refused to assume Lisk was the killer without more evidence as those around him clamored for an arrest. In November 1985, after Lisk refused to give a voluntary blood sample, Enterkin obtained a search warrant for a donation Lisk made at a local blood bank. The blood type associated with the semen found inside Tonya and in the towel left by her head was type A, but Lisk's blood came back type O. In the next two decades, this way of clearing suspects would be rendered useless because of DNA testing, but for Enterkin it meant he had to clear Lisk as a suspect and officially bring his investigation to a close after approximately one year.

For all intents and purposes, it was now a cold case.

"I recommend that this case be inactivated pending additional information," Enterkin wrote in his final entry in Tonya's case file on

January 8, 1986. "When the victim was found dead she appeared to be the victim of a rape and homicide. First reports from the pathologists stated that there was no signs of sex. Later reports from the FBI revealed that semen was found on the vaginal slides and also on a towel left at the scene."

❖ ❖ ❖

From November 1986 through the end of 1989, the *Pensacola News Journal* ran paid ads from Crimestoppers every few months that recapped the details of Tonya's case and included a phone number to call with tips.

In 1987, there was one tip called in on the case, which went nowhere. On November 21, 1989, a weekly public access television show called "Police Talk" ran an episode about Tonya's case. The show used local actors and police officers to re-create scenes from unsolved cases in the Pensacola area, and Tonya's case was one of only seven unsolved murders in Pensacola since 1975. The episode produced no new leads and no new tips.

❖ ❖ ❖

Tina Boone was one of the few people with separate connections to Tim Davidson and Tonya. She knew Tim from middle school, back when they rode the same bus, and she knew Tonya through her older sister, Tammy, who was one of Tonya's best friends growing up. Tina and Tammy even attended Tonya's wedding to Michael McKinley in 1978.

As she got older, Tina became close friends with Tonya and because of that got to know Vanita and Renee as well, but Tonya lost touch with most of her old friends during her relationship with Tim. By 1985, it had been several years since Tina or Tammy had been in regular contact with Tonya, and they were both living in Jacksonville when they received news she had been murdered.

"Tonya was one of our oldest, best friends," Tina said. "We were devastated."

By 1989, Tina was living back in Pensacola and out with friends one night at a bar called The Red Baron when she saw a familiar face on the other side of the room. It was Tim, with a pretty blonde sitting on his lap. Tina waited for the girl to go to the restroom and then went over and greeted Tim with a hug. When the blonde came back from the restroom, she was visibly agitated at the sight of Tim talking to another woman before Tina realized she recognized her as well.

"For a second I thought me and this woman were about to get into a fight," Tina said. "Then I realized it was Vanita so I was like 'Hey, it's me, it's Tina Boone,' and she was like 'Well, hey … ' and the moment she realized it was me you could tell it freaked her the fuck out. They left within a few minutes."

Tina's mind was reeling. As far as she knew, Vanita was still married to Larry Winchester, and Tim was not only Tonya's ex and the father of her child but one of Larry's best friends. Shortly after Tim and Vanita left, a man at the bar asked Tina how she knew Tim and Vanita.

"You know they killed a girl, right?" the man asked her. "Those two. Everybody here knows it. They had some guy around here do it, but they were the ones who had that girl killed."

The words made Tina feel sick to her stomach.

"This person didn't know me," she said. "He didn't know I knew Tonya and she was one of my oldest, best friends. It makes me start shaking again just thinking about it."

Tina said she called the police the next day and relayed her story. There is a report of a call to the Crimestoppers hotline in 1989 in an official police report, but it doesn't reference what the tip pertained to or any other information about who may have called it in. Tina never heard back from the police.

❖ ❖ ❖

Tim spent the first few years after Tonya's murder navigating being a single father with family and friends always ready and willing to lend a helping hand. Tim leaned heavily on his older brother, Kelvin, who kept him employed at different times through companies he owned or ran. Tonya's father, Joe Ethridge, was also a constant presence in Tim's life.

While Kelvin felt like he could always tell his younger brother "no" if he wanted to, he was determined to make sure his nephew never had to go without, even if it only seemed to enable bad habits for his brother, which now included full-blown addictions to drugs and alcohol.

"I think it's safe to say he didn't spend another sober day in his life after Tonya was killed," Kelvin said. "He just couldn't deal with it."

By the late 1980s, Vanita and Larry had three sons under 10 years old, and their marriage was slowly disintegrating. According to both Larry and Vanita, the marriage was at its weakest point when Tim showed up on their doorstep with Tim Jr. in tow and looking for a place to stay. Just like Kelvin and Joe Ethridge and so many others, Larry and Vanita would not allow their disdain for Tim's behavior to keep them from helping Tim Jr.

"It's one thing for Tim to show up on his own, and I could tell him to fuck off or whatever, which I had no problem doing," Larry said. "But when kids are involved, it's different. I couldn't turn away [Tim Jr.] because that was part of Tonya and she was my friend and that was her boy. No matter how I felt about Tim."

Tim and Tim Jr. began to stay with Larry and Vanita for extended periods. During this time, Tim cycled through different girlfriends while Vanita took over caring for Tim Jr. alongside her boys, who were all around the same age. According to Vanita, Tim spent many nights sobbing and telling her how unfair it was that people still thought he killed Tonya when he had nothing to do with it. He cried so much over it that eventually Vanita believed he was telling the truth. Larry believed Tim was innocent, too, but for different reasons.

"I never thought he killed her, because he was a coward," Larry said. "I knew he just didn't have it in him to take a life."

Larry's construction job took him out of town for weeks at a time to Biloxi, Mississippi, which was about a two-hour drive from Pensacola. Like Tim, Larry was dealing with addiction, although Larry's focus was almost entirely on making the perfect batch of crystal meth in his garage. Larry treated his addiction to crystal like most people treated their hobbies.

"I liked to just disappear into the garage," Larry said. "When I could do that, it kind of became my whole world."

At some point during one of Larry's work trips, Tim and Vanita began having an affair. Larry admitted he was having affairs when he was out of town, so it made Vanita feel less guilty about cheating, regardless of who she was cheating with. When the affair got too intense, Tim said he moved to Orlando with Tim Jr. for one year to "get away from Vanita" but eventually returned to Pensacola and resumed the affair. One day, Tim told Vanita he was going to move to Indiana, where he had family who could help raise Tim Jr., and he wanted her to come with him.

The next time Larry went to Biloxi to work for a few weeks, Vanita told him she was going to help Tim with the move to Indiana and then return home on her own. Her actual plan was to leave Larry for good and take their sons with her. She was willing to roll the dice on her future and her children's future with a man she'd seen physically and mentally abuse Tonya for years.

"I didn't think of the abuse because that's not what I saw when he came back around," Vanita said. "I just saw this kind of weak, broken person. He was devastated. It was two or three years later, and he still couldn't get over the fact that Tonya was gone. He seemed like a completely different person."

Larry said he came home from Biloxi to find the couple's oldest son, 10-year-old Larry Jr., alone and crying on the front steps. Larry Jr. said he'd been told he wasn't allowed to go on the trip to Indiana. Later, Vanita said it was Larry Jr.'s decision not to go.

After two more weeks and no contact from Tim, Vanita or the other children, Larry finally got in touch with Vanita over the phone. He asked her if she was "with Tim now," and she said she was. Larry told her he wanted his other two sons back, and Vanita said they were staying with her.

One month later, as they prepared for a visit from Tim's family, Tim and Vanita began to argue. Tim punched Vanita and broke her nose. It was the first time he'd ever hit her. After Tim's family left and the argument continued, he punched her again. Later, after Tim fell asleep, Vanita called Larry and tearfully asked if she and their two sons could come back to Pensacola. Larry said the boys were welcome to come home. She was not.

"You made your fucking bed with that piece of shit," Larry said. "Now sleep in it."

Vanita, filled with regret over her decision to leave her home and her husband, now found herself in the same cycle of abuse, separation and reconciliation that Tonya had been in until just days before her murder.

Tim and Vanita moved frequently, dragging the three young boys with them all over the country. Twice over the next decade, Vanita left and moved in with her sister in the Chicago area. Both times she and Tim reconciled. For Vanita, the reason was always because it was the path of least resistance. The easiest thing to do was slip back into her life with Tim and the boys.

❈ ❈ ❈

In August 1991, Tonya's case was back in the news after police in Gulfport, Mississippi, arrested 35-year-old drifter Donald Leroy Evans for the kidnapping, rape and murder of 10-year-old Beatrice Louise Routh. Routh's mother, Tami Giles, let Evans pay her to bring her daughter home for sex with a promise to return her after he was done. Evans took Beatrice back to his trailer, where he raped her. Afterward, when she said she was going to tell on him, he killed her.

After Evans led police to Routh's body, he confessed to having killed 70 more people in 17 states over the previous decade, including Florida. Tonya's murder and Patricia Stephens' murder were two of four cases in the Pensacola area that law enforcement looked at after Evans' confession. Out of the 70 rapes and murders Evans confessed to, only three resulted in convictions and none of them was in Pensacola.

In 1993, Evans received the death penalty for Beatrice Routh's murder. In 1999, he was stabbed to death in the shower by a fellow death row inmate.

❈ ❈ ❈

Larry and Vanita's divorce was finalized in the spring of 1993, right around when Tim and Vanita moved back to Pensacola. According to Vanita, Tonya was a frequent topic of discussion during her relationship with Tim and usually came up when alcohol or drugs were involved.

"The wrong person died," Tim said to Vanita. "It should have been you."

"The best thing she ever did was leave your ass," Vanita replied. "You probably killed her and now you're probably gonna kill me."

When they moved back to Pensacola, Vanita's family got a firsthand look at Tim's abuse.

One time, during a day at Pensacola Beach with her older sister, Deb Adkins, Vanita fought with Tim over a necklace she was wearing he thought was given to her by another man. When Tim snatched the necklace off her neck, Vanita fought back, and the police had to intervene. After Adkins picked Vanita up at the police station and brought her back to Tim, he started yelling at both of them. Adkins made it clear she wouldn't allow him to talk with her like that.

"He backed down and apologized for talking smart to me, but he was always in trouble and he was always a lowlife," Adkins said. "I can't tell you how happy I was when my sister finally got away from him for good. I think we all always thought he was the one who killed Tonya."

Tim was arrested in Pensacola for DUI in the summer of 1994 — the first of four DUI arrests in Pensacola over the next decade. After the fourth DUI, Tim's driving privileges were permanently revoked, although he was arrested two more times for driving on a suspended license. Tim was charged with one felony count of aggravated stalking in 1996, and in 1997 he was charged with one felony count of battery.

Tim believed he had a foolproof way of keeping himself out of prison. He believed this because it worked pretty much every time he needed it to.

"He would bring me to every little court case with him," Tim Jr. said. "And he'd tell the judge, 'I'm a single father, I can't go to jail because who's going to take care of my son?' And the judge would always fall for it. Then we'd go back and do it all over again. Look ... I knew that he loved me. He was never physically violent toward me. I also always knew he was very selfish. I always knew that he worried about himself more than anybody else."

10

THE SHOEBOX

Tim Jr. didn't learn the truth about how his mother died until he was 14 years old.

He learned the truth one day while snooping through his father and Vanita's closet. He found a shoebox that contained a handwritten letter from Vanita to the producers of "The Montel Williams Show" with details from Tonya's murder and a request for her case to be featured on an upcoming episode about psychics who claimed they could help solve cold case murders. Up until that point, Tim Jr. believed his mother died in a car accident, because that was the story he'd been told by his father and Vanita his entire life. When they returned home that day, Tim Jr. confronted them with the letter, and they told him some version of the truth.

One of the reasons Tim and Vanita were able to keep the lie going for so long was that, except for his grandfather, Tim Jr. was kept almost entirely away from Tonya's side of the family. Joe Ethridge, who died in 2000, was so permanently scarred by his daughter's murder that he never spoke of her or what happened to her. The only time Tim Jr. ever heard anyone talk to his grandfather about his mother was when Joe Ethridge was on his deathbed and Tim swore to the dying man he had nothing to do with his daughter's death.

Tim Jr.'s memory of his mother was mostly formed by stories from his uncle, Kelvin, who had been close friends with Tonya. These were the stories Tim Jr. cherished the most and the ones he thought came the closest to him getting to know his mother. From Kelvin, Tim learned Tonya was generous and happy. He learned she was a kind person who had no real enemies and made friends easily.

"Everybody liked her," Tim Jr. said. "She was pretty and she was tall and she made friends wherever she went. And my uncle always made clear that she loved me very, very much. He said I was everything to her."

❖ ❖ ❖

Vanita and Tim saw each other for the last time in the early 2000s, although no one who was there that night remembers exactly what year.

After a fight, Vanita threw a drunken Tim out of the house and went to bed. Later that night, Tim found his way back into the house and crept into Vanita's bedroom while everyone was asleep. Vanita woke up to Tim with his hands around her throat. Vanita fought back, and the commotion woke Tim Jr., who was now a 6-foot-3, 200-pound teenager. He ran into Tim and Vanita's bedroom and saw his father on top of Vanita, where he seemed to be trying to choke her to death.

"[Tim Jr.] picked him up and slammed him on the floor ... bodyslammed him," Vanita said. "Then he picked him up again and threw him out the door. I got in my car and left and didn't come back that night. The next day I woke up and had marks all over my throat. It had happened a couple of times before, where he'd tried to choke me, but not like this. This time I actually thought he was trying to kill me."

It was the first time Tim Jr. ever physically stood up to his father, and his being there that night may very well have saved Vanita's life. Following the incident, father and son broke off contact for the first time.

One year later, Tim Jr. was enlisted in the Air Force, and Vanita was in a new relationship, in another place with another man. Tim stayed in Pensacola.

❖ ❖ ❖

In October 1992, Carolynn Stephens reached out to the FBI for help in clearing suspects in Tonya's case through DNA testing for the first time. The first sample Stephens sent to the FBI was from Lisk, who was still considered the top suspect even though he'd been cleared in 1985 when his blood type was found to be different from the blood type of semen found in Tonya's body. Eight months later, in June 1993, the FBI informed Stephens that Lisk's DNA was not a match.

By the early 2000s, Stephens no longer needed help from the FBI for DNA testing. The process now went through the Florida Department of Law Enforcement and no longer took eight months to get results back. In 2004, Stephens ran much more in-depth tests on the forensic evidence in Tonya's case, including a new round of DNA tests for Lisk and a first round of DNA testing for Tim. Just like in 1993, Lisk wasn't a match. Neither was Tim, which meant there was now irrefutable proof he had nothing to do with Tonya's murder.

RENEESASSY@AOL.COM

In the year following her younger sister's murder, Renee Ethridge made weekly visits to the Pensacola Police Department to receive updates on the case. After James Enterkin recommended his investigation be declared inactive in January 1986 and it became relegated to the department's cold case file, Renee was told to communicate exclusively through phone calls. Sometimes, she still just showed up.

In her personal life, Renee was quiet to the point of being considered meek. When it came to seeking justice for Tonya, it was the opposite. Her anger and determination grew in ways she couldn't anticipate as over and over again she was told she just needed to move on. Hearing that always pissed her off.

Move on? Fuck that.

"Was I annoying? Sure. Did I make people uncomfortable? Sure. Did I care? Absolutely not," Renee said.

In 2001, Renee set up her first email account at ReneeSassy@aol.com. One of the first people Renee reached out to was Vanita, asking for Tim Jr.'s contact information.

"Sorry it took me so long to get back to you about Timothy's phone number," Vanita wrote back on August 2, 2001. "Here it is ... I didn't even send him a birthday card. That is the first time since he was born that I missed it. He probably didn't even notice though. I'm sure Kelvin and the Cleavers (Ha) made up for it. I just hope Tim sent him one. I wish today were Friday. I am so tired this week. We put up insulation and new walls in the spare bedroom last weekend, and this weekend we will redo the whole bathroom. I didn't realize how tiring it could be to be in a normal relationship. But I like it. Are you in your mom's trailer in Jay? Where does she live? Lorinda has a gorgeous home. It has five bedrooms and four bathrooms. Must be nice. She did well by marrying Tom, but she doesn't treat him good. Don't mention I said that though. Gotta go finish getting ready for work. It takes me over an hour, and I wake up Al at 6:45 and he is out the door by 7??????? Talk to you soon, Vanita."

Email allowed Renee to contact law enforcement anytime she wanted, and she took full advantage. On February 12, 2003, a veteran detective replied to an email from Renee. It was Ted Chamberlain, the same detective who convinced James Enterkin to take another run at Tonya's case when he was ready to declare it inactive in the fall of 1985.

"I am sorry it took so long to get back with you," Chamberlain wrote. "I am working a homicide case that is 26 years old at this time and I feel I am very close to an arrest. At this time I have not had time to look at your sister's case. I hope I can get to it before I retire. We do not have anyone that just works cold cases. I am the closest thing to it. I still have to work on cases that are assigned to me on the west side. I try to do the best I can. I know your sister's homicide, and I feel I know who did it. I hope I have the time to work on it. Feel free to email me anytime."

For Renee, the email from Chamberlain was a shock to the system. Tim was the only suspect the family were ever told about, and they were never informed he'd passed multiple DNA tests.

"Help!" Renee wrote back the same day. "How is that supposed to make me and my family feel? Knowing the police department has a good idea who killed my sister and don't have time to work on it. Try being in my shoes for a moment. The worst thing that could have been taken from me and my family ... my only sister I had has been taken away from me and my family. She has a son that has lived a rough life not knowing his mother ... has grown up knowing there are just a few people in the world that really care. I haven't lived a single day in the past 18 years that I don't think about that tragic night. I understand that there is not the manpower to help, but where is the justice? I understand your point of view, just please think of mine. I don't fault you but I don't know what else to do now but pray. But I have been doing that from day one. If there is anything I can do to help please tell me. I would be willing to help in any way I can. Thanks for your time and honesty."

Renee also emailed the Escambia County Sheriff's Office, which had a separate unit that worked specifically on cold cases. The ECSO cold case unit responded to Renee to tell her she needed to go through the Pensacola police. When Renee hadn't heard from the police in almost a year, she reached out to Pensacola police chief John Mathis, asking if Chamberlain had retired and if Mathis could see about getting Tonya's case featured on the Florida Department of Law Enforcement website under its section on unsolved homicides.

"I remember your sister's tragic murder," Mathis wrote to Renee on September 16, 2008. "Yes, you are correct, that officer did retire ... as you can see I am forwarding your email to Capt. Paul Kelly and will look into your request and get back with you. I am sorry for your loss and lack of closure in this matter."

Kelly emailed Renee shortly afterward to tell her he was looking over the case file and would try to get Tonya's case placed on the FDLE website. What he didn't tell her was he had already decided to reopen the investigation.

"I wanted to let you know that I have been reviewing your sister's case thoroughly and today I met with members of the FDLE lab," Kelly wrote in an email to Renee on September 30, 2008. "We are all very optimistic about the advances that have been made in DNA testing/comparison about your sister's case. We are in the process of resubmitting items that were tested years ago. We hope that these items will lead us to the suspect. I do not want to give you any false hope. But I do want you to know that we are trying to do all that we can to catch the murderer."

On October 10, 2008, Kelly sent a treasure trove of forensic evidence to the FDLE for DNA testing. It was the first official activity on the case outside of DNA testing in 22 years.

By the end of the month, Kelly and Stephens were beginning to clear suspects. This included some people who were previously cleared, including Lisk for the third time and Tim for the second time. For the first time, the DNA from Tonya's case would go into CODIS, the national DNA database run by the FBI that collects DNA from felons in all 50 states.

"Unfortunately, the DNA did not match one of our best suspects, Mr. Lisk," Kelly wrote to Renee on October 27, 2008. "We are not finished though. The FDLE is reexamining all of the evidence to see what they can find. We hope that the DNA profile from the evidence matches with someone in CODIS. If you are not familiar with this database, you can look it up online. It is a great tool for law enforcement. I am also looking at a similar murder in Escambia County, and the investigator is looking into it with me. It occurred two months after Tonya's murder. We are trying to determine if the evidence in Tonya's case matches that case. We will keep you informed."

Renee wrote back a few days later.

"Thank you for keeping me informed," she wrote. "You will never know how much I appreciate all that you are doing. Actually, some hope is better than no hope at all, which I have felt like this is a hopeless situation for a long time. Thank you for all you do. Can you refresh my memory on Mr. Lisk? I know the name but am unsure."

⑫

RABBIT HOLE

As a longtime television reporter at ABC affiliate WEAR-TV in Pensacola, Mollye Barrows had a reputation for consistently taking the time to research, develop and air stories on local cold cases, which was almost wholly unique for a reporter on Florida's Gulf Coast. More specifically, she had a knack for getting family members of victims to talk with her about the worst thing that ever happened to most of them, which was no small task.

After Renee emailed and told her about Kelly reopening Tonya's case, Barrows put together a report that aired on the 23rd anniversary of the murder. The report featured an interview with Renee and pointed out the similarities between her murder and the murder of Patricia Stephens two months later. It churned up several leads. The first was from Tina Boone, who contacted Kelly about her experience at the Red Baron Lounge in 1989 when she ran into Vanita and Tim, who were in the midst of an affair at the time. Boone relayed the story of the man who told her Vanita and Tim had Tonya killed. She said the man's name was Charles Smith, and he may have lived in Gulf Breeze.

Kelly went with another veteran detective, Chuck Mallett, to interview Smith at the auto body shop where he worked, but Smith didn't have a great recollection of a conversation he may or may not have had at a bar 20 years prior. He did, however, remember Tonya's murder and remembered the rumors about Tim and Vanita having her killed.

❈ ❈ ❈

Vanita called Kelly in January 2009 after she heard about Barrows' report airing on the anniversary of Tonya's death. Vanita told Kelly she hoped the murder could still be solved and gave him details about her relationship with Tim. She said they lived together on and off for 15 years and he began to physically abuse her from one month after she left her husband until the end of the relationship. On several occasions, she said Tim strangled her until she passed out.

Vanita said she accused Tim of killing Tonya on "many occasions," even though she knew he had an alibi and he always denied having anything to do with the murder. Unprompted, Vanita added that she pretty much raised Tim Jr. on her own and that the affair with Tim didn't begin until several years after Tonya's murder. There were parts of Vanita's story in 2009 that differed from her initial account but could be chalked up to a faulty memory. When she spoke with police in 1985, she said she waited in the parking lot at Ritchie's Lounge on December 30, the night before the murder, until Tonya returned to the bar several hours later and she'd driven them home. In 2009, Vanita said she left the bar and Tonya received a ride home from someone else and didn't come back until early the next morning. Vanita said she was pretty sure Tonya took rides home from strangers regularly and without asking too many questions.

Vanita's last request during her conversation with Kelly was to make sure Tim did not learn her new whereabouts, because she was "happy and living in California with her new husband."

❈ ❈ ❈

Jeffrey Brunt became a key suspect during Enterkin's initial investigation because of his changing alibi and suspicious, hostile behavior during questioning. After reading about his involvement with the case, Kelly thought it would be a good idea to meet with him face-to-face.

On January 16, 2009, Kelly went to Brunt's home to speak with him and ask him to submit a cheek swab for DNA testing, which Brunt agreed to right away. Brunt was just 19 years old when he'd first been approached by the police in 1985 — he was now 43 years old and considerably worse for the wear. Brunt told Kelly he worked at Darryl's for just three or four months before he quit and, just like in 1985, he denied any involvement in Tonya's murder. Because he lived in the neighborhood where Tonya's body was found, Brunt told Kelly he was privy to the rumors floating around at the time involving himself as well as others.

One of them piqued Kelly's interest.

✿ ✿ ✿

For a long time, Brunt said, a persistent rumor in the neighborhood was the son of the owner of a local pet grooming salon murdered Tonya. While Brunt couldn't remember where he first heard the rumor or the name of the son, he did remember the son had an affair with the wife of one of his friends, Jeffrey Macht.

The name of the pet grooming business was Universal Pet Salon and was owned by Stephen Lincourt and his ex-wife, Becky Lincourt. Stephen died of a brain aneurysm in 2006, at 52 years old. When Kelly spoke with Becky, she said she was married to Stephen from 1978 to 1992 and had little to do with his business during their marriage. Much later, she learned Stephen was having affairs with several of his employees.

During their marriage, Becky said she and Stephen lived on Peacock Drive with her daughter from a previous marriage and remembered waking up on New Year's Day 1985 and seeing her street full of police cars after Tonya's body was found. Becky remembered Brunt's friend, Jeffrey Macht, and his wife, Kim Macht, because Kim worked for her husband. One key detail Becky left out — and something Kelly knew before they spoke — was that a fourth person had also lived at the home on Peacock Drive. That person was her 20-year-old son from a previous marriage, Brian Tullis Williams, who had a long criminal history in Pensacola dating back to the 1980s that included arrests for snatch-and-grab robberies, church break-ins, drug posses-sion and, finally, a felony conviction for burglary in the early 2000s while on probation for another felony. Williams' final conviction clas-sified him as a habitual offender in Florida and came with a manda-tory 15-year prison sentence.

From this, Kelly could only conclude the rumor Brunt heard about the son of the owner of a dog grooming business referred to Williams, who was Stephen Lincourt's stepson at the time.

❖ ❖ ❖

Kelly found an address for Jeffrey Macht in Milton and left a busi-ness card with relatives who were living there. When they eventually spoke, Macht said in the early 1980s his social circle included Brunt, Stephen Lincourt and Tom Majors, who owned American Kennels in Pensacola. Macht said his wife, Kim, went to work for Stephen shortly after they moved to Pensacola in 1981 but didn't mention whether he'd been cuckolded by Stephen's stepson.

Majors' ex-wife, Brita Reynolds, said she'd seen her husband using drugs with Stephen in the mid-1980s and that it was common knowledge that Stephen "fooled around" on his wife while he owned Universal Pet Salon and the family lived on Peacock Drive. Within weeks, DNA tests on Brunt's cheek swab cleared him as a suspect. Kelly notified the FBI he needed a DNA comparison for Williams' DNA in CODIS. Within weeks, they reported back that Williams wasn't a match.

❖ ❖ ❖

As Kelly's investigation moved forward, each new suspect in Tonya's murder seemed to top the last when it came to their previous evil deeds.

In February 2009, Kelly received information on Tonya's case he was told originated from a confidential intelligence report — com-monly known as a "snitch file" — from the Escambia County Sheriff's Office. The report identified Joe William Charron Jr., 43 years old, as a suspect in Tonya's murder. The source was a confidential informant in another, separate case, a woman called Heather, who was identified as a relative of Joe Jr.'s stepmother, Bonnie Charron. Heather was willing to speak with Kelly as long as she could remain anonymous. She had a twisted story to tell.

✿ ✿ ✿

In the late 1970s, Joe Charron Sr. was the full-time youth minister at Pensacola Baptist Temple and Bonnie was the church pianist when the two began an extramarital affair. Joe Sr. had a reputation for being strict and overly dogmatic when it came to teaching the Bible and following its rules, so when it was discovered he and Bonnie were having sex, they were both thrown out of the church.

After their exit, Joe Sr. and Bonnie divorced their respective spouses and married each other. They combined their two families in one home, with Bonnie's two daughters from her previous marriage and Joe Sr.'s two daughters and one son, Joe Jr., from his previous marriage. The family lived together in a home close to Peacock Drive in the mid-1980s, which was a time Heather said she was making regular visits to Bonnie at the home. Heather said things seemed to be in a state of constant turmoil because of conflicts between the children and their parents.

On one of the visits, in early 1985, Heather found Bonnie sitting in the kitchen, alone, trembling and visibly upset after eavesdropping on a conversation between Joe Jr. and a friend. That day, Bonnie told Heather she heard Joe Jr. tell his friend that he and two other boys grabbed a girl off the street and dragged her to a wooded area where Joe Jr. held the girl down while the other boys took turns raping her. Afterward, Joe Jr. said, they realized she was going to tell on them so they killed her and threw her body on the side of the road close to Scenic Highway.

Bonnie said she didn't know what to do with the information because it was her stepson. By all accounts, she never told anyone else what she heard after that day.

Joe Jr. moved out for his final semester of high school in Pensacola and graduated in 1986. Shortly after graduation, Joe Jr. moved to Dallas with his best friend, Andy Huntress, but the two moved back to Pensacola six months later. After they returned from Dallas, Joe Jr. met his first wife, Dawn Douglas, at the Pensacola Bible Institute in 1987. They were married for a decade, and after the marriage ended, Dawn moved in with Joe Sr. and Bonnie and worked at the business they owned, Countryside Party Particular. To make things even more confusing, Dawn's brother, Don Douglas, married one of Bonnie's daughters, Sherra, who was Dawn's best friend. When Kelly went to Pensacola Baptist Temple to talk to churchgoers who knew Joe Sr. and Bonnie before their affair, he was told it was common knowledge in the church community that once their families moved in together, Joe Jr. had been accused of sexually abusing Bonnie's daughters.

Kelly found Huntress living in Wiley, Texas, where local police obtained a DNA sample and got him on the phone to speak with Kelly. Huntress said he met Joe Jr. at Pensacola Baptist Temple when they were both six years old but lost contact in middle school after Joe Sr. was thrown out of the church. The two reconnected during their senior year of high school after Joe Jr. moved out on his own, which led to the two of them moving to Texas for a short time.

When Joe Jr. and Huntress returned to Pensacola, they rented an apartment together and Joe Jr. worked at Goofy Golf, a miniature golf course in Pensacola owned by a family he knew from his time at Pensacola Baptist Temple. Joe Jr.'s boss at Goofy Golf was Julia Boothe, who ran the business for her family. Boothe said her son, Richard Boothe, was close friends with both Joe Jr. and Huntress around the time of Tonya's murder.

Joe Sr. had been the youth pastor for all three boys growing up at Pensacola Baptist Temple.

"Andy Huntress was wild," Julia said. "Joe Jr. was a sweet boy. Not violent in any way, but I felt like Andy seemed jealous of Joe Jr.'s girlfriend."

The group, which included Huntress and Joe Jr.'s girlfriends at the time, weren't exactly high achievers. Their regular spots to hang out were Goofy Golf, the clay pits on Cerny Street, the Muscogee River and occasionally Navy Point, a gigantic park in Pensacola right on Pensacola Bay. Their main activities were drinking heavily and smoking copious amounts of marijuana, along with occasional cocaine use.

Richard Boothe said he lost contact with Joe Jr. for a brief period but reconnected in 1987, when Joe Jr. asked him to come to the apartment he shared with his girlfriend so they could set him up with one of their female neighbors. When Richard showed up, he discovered the woman was disabled, which infuriated him. Richard said he never saw Joe Jr. again after that night, although he heard Joe Jr.'s girlfriend left him and joined the military when she discovered he couldn't pay rent because he was spending all of his paychecks on alcohol and drugs. Richard said he didn't think Joe Jr. could have hurt anyone based on the time they spent together.

"People change over the years," Richard said. "I know he did."

By 2009, Joe Jr. was on probation and required to check in with a parole officer at least once a day, although he had yet to submit a DNA sample for CODIS, even though it was required of convicted felons. After going to Joe Jr.'s address several times and finding no one there, Kelly got word he was in Santa Rosa County Jail on a probation violation and had him submit to a DNA test. Within the next month, Kelly cleared Richard Boothe, Andy Huntress and, finally, Joe Jr. as suspects in Tonya's murder through DNA testing.

The investigation rolled on.

✿ ✿ ✿

Kelly stayed busy with Tonya's case through the first half of 2009, first off the tip from Brunt about the possible connection to a local dog grooming salon, then by the discovery of the confidential file at the Escambia County Sheriff's Office which named Joe Jr. as a suspect. Both ended up being rabbit holes. Kelly also had to sift his way through a growing volley of accusations Tonya's family and friends were lobbing at each other.

Kelly found out through Larry Winchester that Tim was telling people a detective in Pensacola told him he knew who killed Tonya and that the detective promised to tell him who it was after he retired. Tim was also telling people that either Kurt Lisk or the unnamed male exotic dancer from Gulf Breeze was probably who killed Tonya. Both Larry and Renee told Kelly they were suspicious of the affair between Vanita and Tim and believed it may have been tied to Tonya's murder in some way. Renee also told Kelly she thought Tonya had briefly hooked up with her ex-husband, Michael McKinley, around the time she got pregnant with Tim Jr., and she believed he might be the biological father.

Kelly followed up with the three people who found Tonya's body on Peacock Drive — Mary Lloyd, her daughter, Sharon Edwards and Sherry's boyfriend at the time, Jeffrey Pierce. All of their stories were unchanged from the statements they gave to police in 1985.

On the night of June 1, 2009, Tim called Kelly and decided to spill his guts. He said it was obvious the police were taking more DNA samples than they needed, so it didn't seem like they were singling out one person, which he believed was Lisk. Then Tim began to fling accusations at almost everyone who was in the vicinity of Tonya when she was killed.

"Larry had no conscience or morals," Tim said. "I think he may have killed Tonya."

Tim kept spilling. He said he began a "sexual affair" with Vanita shortly after Tonya died but moved to Orlando with Tim Jr. specifically to "get away from Vanita," because she was still married. When Tim returned to Pensacola after one year, he and Vanita resumed their affair and she eventually left Larry to be with him. Kelly already had most of this information.

"Vanita was the worst mistake of my life," Tim said. "The fucking worst decision I ever made."

In 2009, Tim was living in a succession of extended-stay hotels in the shittier parts of Pensacola and had an infant daughter with a woman he'd just gotten out of a long-term relationship with. Tim said he knew Vanita was living in California with her new husband, which Kelly already knew as well.

Tim said when he spoke with him, Larry lied and said he hadn't spoken to the police in years. Tim tried to bad-mouth the police to get Larry to open up, but he continued to lie. Tim wanted to know what Kelly thought about Larry being deceptive.

"Don't worry about it," Kelly said. "And stay out of the investigation."

"You're being an asshole," said Tim, who began to cry. "You're just being a real asshole to me for some reason."

"Who killed Tonya?" Kelly asked. "Tell me, Tim. Who killed her?"

"I don't know," Davidson said between sobs. "I really don't."

In August 2009, Tim's mother called Kelly to tell him she'd been contacted by several people who said they gave DNA samples to the police as part of his investigation. Like her son, she was ready to share theories on who killed Tonya, saying she always believed Larry and Vanita were behind it but couldn't explain why. She also told Kelly that Tim was in jail again, serving a one-year sentence for violating his probation and driving with a suspended license. She wanted to see if he could help Tim get out early, but Kelly decided that, at least for now, Tim was fine right where he was.

❋ ❋ ❋

In January 2010, Kelly received a call from officials at the Escambia County Road Prison who oversaw a group of "trusted inmates" allowed to clean up trash along local roads during the day. At the time, Tim was one of those inmates and had gone to one of the officers in private to tell them another inmate, Dion Booker, had information about Tonya's murder. Tim said he and Booker had several confrontations at a bar called Gene's Lounge in the mid-1980s over Tonya, who worked with Booker at a Waffle House. Tim said Booker admitted he had sex with Tonya several times and while he hadn't said anything to incriminate himself in Tonya's murder, Tim still wanted Kelly to check him out.

Booker said he recognized Tim almost immediately when he showed up on the prison road crew because he remembered meeting him through Vanita and Tonya. He also remembered Tonya showing up at a friend's apartment with a busted lip and bruised ribs after Tim beat her up. Booker denied having sex with Tonya but confirmed he and Tim had several confrontations at Gene's Lounge and added there was another confrontation while they were on a camping trip to Pensacola Beach with a large group of people. That time, Booker said Tim pulled a knife on him. Booker said he was in jail when Tonya was murdered, which Kelly was able to confirm quickly.

❋ ❋ ❋

On May 6, 2010, Escambia County Sheriff's Office investigator Mark Smeester approached Kelly with another possible lead in Tonya's case. Smeester said he received information that John David Stewart Jr., who was convicted of sexual crimes twice in Pensacola in the late 1980s, may have been involved with Tonya's murder.

After Kelly went over Stewart's file, he contacted the Hill County (Texas) Sheriff's Office and learned Stewart died by suicide in 1999 after police showed up at Stewart's house to arrest him for sexual battery. Standing in his doorway as the police walked up the front steps, Stewart put a shotgun in his mouth and blew his own head off. Kelly found out there was still enough physical evidence available to obtain a sample of Stewart's DNA and arranged to have it sent from Texas to Florida for testing.

In July, Kelly located Stewart's ex-wife Ashley who said she was married to Stewart from 1980 to 1984. Ashley told Kelly she agreed to meet Stewart at his home shortly after they separated so she could get some items for their 3-year-old son. Once inside, Stewart attacked her from behind, punching and choking her until she lost consciousness. Ashley came to with a broken nose and a broken jaw as Stewart dragged her into a bedroom to rape her. As their son watched and screamed, Stewart held a knife to Ashley's throat and tore her clothes off.

"If I can't have you, no one will," he said.

Stewart couldn't get an erection, so he beat Ashley some more before he let her go. Once she got somewhere safe, she called the police but Stewart, a local firefighter, wasn't charged. In December 1984 — the same month Tonya was murdered — police arrested Stewart after Ashley's sister walked in on him trying to rape Ashley after he'd broken into her house.

In March 1985 — the same month Patricia Stephens was murdered — Stewart tried to run Ashley off the road with his truck. When he cornered her, she locked the doors and honked on the horn repeatedly to scare him away.

Ashley said Stewart always carried a pocketknife and was an expert at tying knots from his time in the Navy. She said he held a gun to her head several times during their marriage, and once, while visiting Dallas, Stewart attacked her in front of some of his family members.

When Stewart's brother stepped in to protect Ashley, Stewart responded by getting a shotgun out of his car and forcing everyone who was outside into the house. Once inside, Stewart woke up everyone who was sleeping and forced them all into one room, where he held them at gunpoint for several hours.

After her divorce from Stewart was finalized, Ashley moved to South Florida with her son and broke off all contact with Stewart and his family. A few weeks before he killed himself, Stewart somehow found her phone number and they spoke for the first time in almost a decade. Two weeks later she learned he was dead.

Kelly tracked down Stewart's second ex-wife, Leah, at her job in Pensacola. When he said Stewart's full name out loud, he saw her face change from curiosity to fear. Leah said she was married to Stewart for 13 months, from February 22, 1987, to March 22, 1988, and only remembered the exact date the divorce went through because it was the same day Stewart was sentenced to 22 years in prison for multiple rapes, attempted murder and aggravated assault.

✵ ✵ ✵

On July 23, 1987, Stewart used a fake name to lure a cleaning woman to an empty apartment in Pensacola. Once inside, he subdued her and raped her. Afterward, he asked her if there was a reason he shouldn't kill her, to which she said he didn't need to kill her because she hadn't seen his face. Stewart dragged her to a room and told her not to leave or he'd kill her. After waiting long enough to make sure Stewart was gone, she drove herself to the hospital and called the police.

Just over two months later, on October 1, Stewart used another fake name to lure a cleaning woman to his own home. As she was cleaning, he attacked her from behind with a hunting knife, but the woman was able to fight back and escape. Police arrested Stewart several weeks later, but he posted a $10,000 bond and was free the next day.

On December 8, 1987, Stewart struck for the third time in less than five months. This time he lured a real estate agent to a rental house four doors down from where he lived by pretending to be a potential homebuyer. Midway through the tour of the home, he attacked. Stewart punched the real estate agent in the face repeatedly, knocking out several of her teeth and breaking her jaw. He wrapped a long sock around her neck, dragged her into another room and raped her. Afterward, he repeatedly threatened to kill her and tried to put her in handcuffs, but she resisted. As Stewart held a knife to her breast, the woman offered him her jewelry and $200 in cash she had in her purse. When he showed no interest in either, she realized he intended to kill her so she grabbed the blade of the knife and a struggle ensued. After the blade snapped off in her hand, the woman began screaming that her husband would be there any second, and Stewart fled.

Stewart was on the run for a week before he called his wife and told her to meet him at the Gainesville airport, and she immediately called the police to inform them where he was. Stewart was confronted by plainclothes officers at the airport but somehow managed to escape and make it to his vehicle. He led authorities on a wild car chase through three counties that only ended when he slammed his vehicle into a police car.

In the short time they were married, Leah said Stewart was regularly violent toward her. On multiple occasions, he threatened her with knives. On multiple occasions, he choked her until she passed out. The day before Stewart raped the real estate agent, Leah said, he tried to rape her at knifepoint but couldn't get an erection.

During their marriage, Stewart told Leah he was in the U.S. Navy Reserves and went on a lot of weekend trips by himself. She later found out this was almost completely a lie but didn't know where he'd gone on those trips. From the end of 1985 through the end of 1987, Stewart lived with Leah in a house at Scenic Highway and Baywoods Drive — just one mile north of where Tonya's body was found on Peacock Drive — and they owned a dog with black hair. She said Stewart blamed his issues on his mother, who he said tried to kill him and his sister when they were children by placing them in a running car in a closed garage before Stewart broke free and got help.

Stewart served 10 years of his 22-year sentence and was only out of prison for two years when he killed himself. When Kelly informed Leah that Stewart was dead, he could see a visible sense of relief wash over her.

"I've spent the last two decades looking over my shoulder," she said. "He was evil."

In August 2010, Kelly received word from the Florida Department of Law Enforcement about the results of Stewart's DNA testing. It wasn't a match, and another promising lead became a dead end.

❄ ❄ ❄

Kelly put Tonya's case on the back burner for almost five years before a breakthrough in DNA science brought him back. In the summer of 2015, "familial DNA" began being used to trace suspects through family members instead of the one-to-one link of a direct DNA match. However, its use was still limited and at that time could only be used for comparisons with DNA in the national CODIS database. If you were an unknown suspect who wasn't in CODIS but had a family member who was a convicted felon and already in the database, it would result in a hit on the felon's DNA sample.

In August 2015, Kelly met with the FDLE and the State Attorney's office to go over the results of a familial DNA match in Tonya's murder. This match showed Daniel Farmer Jr., a 29-year-old Jacksonville man with a conviction for cocaine trafficking, was somehow related to the suspect in Tonya's murder. Kelly identified eight of Farmer's male relatives in the Jacksonville area who fit into the suspected age range of Tonya's killer and within days was making the six-hour drive east to find out what they were all doing on December 31, 1984.

❄ ❄ ❄

Kelly's first point of contact in Jacksonville was Daniel Jr.'s grandmother, Carol Anne Dover, who was married to Daniel Jr.'s grandfather, Ed, from 1962 to 1977. Carol Anne and Ed had two children together — David in 1965 and Daniel Jr.'s father, Daniel Sr., in 1966. After their divorce, Carole Anne stayed in close contact with Ed because of the children they shared and because he worked at the same Jacksonville Winn-Dixie warehouse as her new husband.

Carol Anne said Ed, who died in 2009, was arrested in 1985 but couldn't remember the circumstances. She got both of her sons to come to her house, and they both agreed to submit DNA samples to Kelly on the spot. David said he lived with his mother after his parents' divorce until he graduated from high school in 1983, then he moved in with his father to be closer to Jacksonville University, where he was attending college. David said he'd never been to Pensacola and didn't think his father or younger brother had either.

Daniel Sr. graduated from high school in 1985 and got a job at the same Winn-Dixie warehouse as his father and stepfather, where he worked until it shut down in 2000. He also remembered the details of his father's arrest in 1985. Daniel Sr. said Ed, who was 44 years old at the time, was dating an 18-year-old girl and after her father found out, there was a confrontation. The two men fought, the girl's father ended up in the hospital and Ed was arrested for assault.

Ed's two brothers, Johnnie Lee and Buck, worked building roads and traveled extensively throughout the state but were both dead. Buck had three sons, Louis, Billy Joe and Jeffrey, and lived with his daughter, Theresa, until he died. When Kelly asked if she still had any of her father's items that might provide a DNA sample, she provided a glass eye. Johnnie Lee's widow agreed to let Kelly use one of his old jackets to take a DNA sample. Kelly obtained a DNA sample from Louis, who told him Billy Joe lived next door but to be careful approaching him.

"What's that supposed to mean?" Kelly asked.

"Well," Louis said. "He's got a temper."

Kelly went next door, and Billy Joe came outside to talk. He said he was in the military but received an honorable discharge in 1979 and was never stationed near Pensacola. Billy Joe said his DNA should already be in CODIS because he had a felony conviction for aggravated battery after he "accidentally" shot a friend in the foot and served 18 months in prison. Billy Joe still willingly gave Kelly a DNA sample. Of the eight male relatives of Daniel Farmer Jr. identified through the original familial DNA connection as possible suspects, Kelly managed to obtain DNA samples from six during his trip to Jacksonville.

In October 2015, the FDLE contacted Kelly to let him know none of the six men matched the DNA from Tonya's killer.

❖ ❖ ❖

In early 2016, Kelly received a call from Detective Robyn Hyatt of the Prince William County (Virginia) Police Department, who said she'd recently received a tip that led her to a transcribed interview with Angela Dover from June 1987 in the Prince William County files. In the interview, Dover said she believed her husband, George Dover, may have been involved in Tonya's murder. According to Angela, George was working as a dishwasher at Darryl's Bar & Grille on New Year's Eve 1984 and walked home from work after his shift was over, which was unusual. Even more unusual? George never went back to Darryl's after New Year's Eve but didn't tell his wife he quit his job for two weeks.

Hyatt said Prince William County reached out to the Pensacola police following Angela's interview in 1987, but Kelly could find no record of that interaction. There was a reference to George among the interviews Enterkin conducted with Darryl's staff, as several people said "George the busboy" was at the after-hours party in the parking lot until dawn. Kelly sent Hyatt a DNA sample from Tonya's killer to compare to a cheek swab from George.

On January 24, 2016, Kelly logged his last entry into the official report, ending his eight-year investigation into Tonya's murder without an arrest.

13

DYING IN SPANISH FORT

Tim Davidson died alone in an assisted living facility in Spanish Fort, Alabama, on January 18, 2013. He was 51 years old and spent the last few years of his life in excruciating physical pain.

A few years before his death, with his body already torn apart from years of drug and alcohol abuse, Tim went to a doctor seeking help with back issues. The doctor not only misdiagnosed Tim with a herniated disc but missed telltale signs of a spinal cord infection, which went untreated and eventually left Tim almost totally paralyzed from the waist down. Tim sued the hospital and received a settlement that gave him some money to live on. By court order, a good chunk of money went into a trust fund for his young daughter. Tim spent the next few years living in extended-stay hotels around Pensacola as his condition worsened. At one point, doctors told Tim he needed to have one of his legs amputated at the knee to prevent the infection in his spine from spreading to the rest of his body, which would almost certainly kill him if it did.

To Tim Jr., who was now married with a son of his own, it seemed like his father just gave up on life.

"His excuse for everything was always that he was paralyzed," Tim Jr. said. "When his doctor told him he would have to amputate his leg just above the knee, [Tim] just told the guy 'I'll die before I let you cut my legs off.' I tried to tell him, you know, 'You have a daughter now and she needs you in her life' but he just didn't care ... he just let his whole life rot away."

Tim Jr. went to Spanish Fort to see his father a few days before he died, but Tim was delirious from pain and didn't recognize his son. Doctors told Tim Jr. the infection had spread to his father's brain. A few days later, he received an early morning phone call from the hospice center to tell him his father had died. Along with Tim Jr., one of the few people around to witness the final, sad years of Davidson's life was Larry Winchester, his former best friend as a teenager and the man Tim stole a wife from decades earlier.

"I wouldn't say that we became friends again, necessarily," Larry said. "It was more just that he needed help ... so I did what I could, which was mainly just driving him around when he was paralyzed. Putting his wheelchair in the back of my truck and taking him wherever he needed to go."

Tim's older brother, Kelvin, reached out to Vanita right before Tim died to let her know about his brother's condition.

"I didn't want to see him, but I did call," Vanita said. "The only thing he really said was 'Well, it took you long enough to call me.'"

Even in death, Tim managed to rub people the wrong way. He was buried in a plot just a few feet from where Tonya was buried at Crain Cemetery in Milton, which enraged Tonya's family, although it was likely partly motivated by wanting to be buried close to his son one day.

Renee, who made weekly visits to her sister's grave, was incensed.

"You won't believe this shit," Renee said as she tended to Tonya's grave. "Even in death, that son of a bitch found a way to bother you."

Renee had a habit of going to Tonya's grave and staying all night after she suspected Tim or some of his family members were stealing from Tonya's grave. One time, someone took black spray paint and drew a stripe directly down the front of the gravestone, right over the picture of Tonya and Tim. No other graves around Tonya's or in the cemetery were defaced.

"[Renee] just had a rough time over the years," said Deb Adkins, who was Renee's cousin and Vanita's older sister. "One of her husbands ran off with another woman, and then her son she had with him was pretty troubled ... then what eventually happened with him was a tragedy as well."

Renee's oldest son, Joey McKinley, battled drug and alcohol addiction throughout his life and was arrested six times from 1997 to 2010 for burglary, drugs and various probation violations. On March 8, 2014, Joey was walking on a rural highway when he was struck by one car and then hit by another car as he lay on the road, still struggling from being hit by the first car. One month later, on the advice of doctors, Renee decided to remove Joey from life support and he died shortly afterward. He was 36 years old, and Renee had him buried next to Tonya at Crain Cemetery in Milton.

"I don't have hope," Renee said a few days after the 34th anniversary of Tonya's murder in January 2019. "I don't have anything to really live for. The thing I look forward to the most is seeing [Tonya and Joey] again after I die. The only thing keeping me going is that I can't give up on finding out what happened to Tonya ... because I know she would never give up on me.

"If I die before I find out, at least I can die knowing I never stopped trying to find out who killed her."

14

CHUCK AND THE MISSING GIRL

After two years of partying at Florida State and the shitty grades to match, Chuck Mallett's father presented him with a choice. He could move home to Pensacola and go to college or stay in Tallahassee and pay his own way at FSU.

Mallett chose the less financially disastrous option and went back home with his tail between his legs, and he enrolled at Pensacola Junior College in the fall of 1988 with no clear idea of what his future might hold. Mallett proceeded to spend much of his free time outside of class wallowing in self-pity, drinking beer with friends and listening to heavy metal in his rusted-out Nissan Sentra.

Mallett was a military brat from a mixed-race family with an American father, James, and a Japanese mother, Akiko. The Malletts were living in Pensacola for the third time following stints when their son was in kindergarten and again in middle school because of his father's commissions in the U.S. Navy. When Mallett graduated from high school in 1986, the family was living in Key West, which ended up being his father's last stop in the Navy before he retired and went to work in the private sector.

One night, while Mallett was sitting with friends at Burger King, a state trooper drove through the parking lot and someone in the group joked about how, since none of them knew what they wanted to do for careers, they should all just become cops. One of Mallett's friends from junior college said there was a cop in one of his classes not much older than them who offered to let him do a ride-along on one of his patrol shifts, but he turned him down. Mallett tracked down the cop, Mike Simmons, and asked if he could take him up on the offer. He was hooked from the first night.

After graduating from the police academy, Mallett was hired by the Pensacola Police Department on August 27, 1990, and placed in the patrol division. He was 22 years old.

One month later, Mallett was in the news for the first time as a cop after he and Simmons found a submerged Chevy Blazer in a Pensacola bayou after the vehicle was reported stolen earlier that day. Mallett was back in the news a few months later when he caught a 39-year-old man, Michael Stapleton, in the process of raping a 15-year-old boy in his car around 4 a.m. In June 1992, Mallett was injured in the line of duty after he fought off a nunchaku-wielding man outside of a local bar. Mallett's instincts quickly won over older cops and created loyalty among his peers. It was a case of someone finding their true calling.

"Even when he was a young officer, he always had that maturity and leadership and intelligence," said Carolynn Stephens, who was hired in 1984, six years before Mallett. "For me, for my position, I just absolutely adored him ... I thought he was a great officer who then became a great supervisor. That respect was always there for him in the building. You could just tell from the beginning."

Mallett and his first wife, Stephanie, had two daughters in the early 1990s: Michelle in 1991 and Jennifer in 1993, around the same time he received his first promotion to detective in the Criminal Investigations Division. Mallett spent one year working on property crimes before spending three years on robberies, rapes, batteries and homicides. These were what police called "crimes against persons" and were regarded as the department's most important cases.

In 1996, Mallett was one of four investigators awarded Certificates of Meritorious Achievement for their work over the previous year. In his first six years as a cop, he developed a reputation for taking on the most difficult cases. If something was deemed too complicated or gruesome for anyone else to handle, it was Mallett who usually got the call. For the generation of cops behind him, Mallett was someone they could look up to. One of those cops was Danny Harnett, who was hired in 1995 and quickly worked his way up to investigations, where he would spend decades teaming up with Mallett to solve cases.

"I looked at Chuck as someone who didn't just want to be good ... he wanted to be the best at what he did," Harnett said. "And that's what I wanted to be. The way I look at it, there's usually a certain percentage of people, say around 5%-10%, who absolutely don't give a shit about what they do or how they do it. Then there's this huge middle where people just want to get by, which is like 70%. They're trying to do the bare minimum. Then there's an upper 15%-20% who really want to excel and be great. That's where Chuck's at. That's where I always wanted to be."

Mallett's reputation for helping solve seemingly unsolvable cases only grew over the years. In 1998, local drug dealer Herman Green was driving in his car with two men in Pensacola, 18-year-old Ricky Hall and Rodriguez Mosley, when he pulled a gun on them and robbed Mosley of $100, shot him and pushed him out of the car. Green drove away with Hall, who was never seen again.

Mallett, on a team led by Detective Pat Doyle, gathered enough evidence and put together a case against Green that the state eventually convicted him of second-degree murder and sentenced him to life in prison without the possibility of parole. As anyone who has ever watched a single episode of "Law & Order" will tell you, getting a conviction without a body is usually impossible.

"I think when it came to homicide cases he worked, that's where you really saw him shine," Harnett said. "It didn't matter what kind. If he was going in on it, he was going to be successful. That's just how he works. And when it's the Super Bowl (of cases), he's going to be suited for that moment."

Mallett and his first wife divorced around the same time he was moving up the ranks in department leadership. The custody hearings were contentious, with Mallett eventually awarded primary custody of their two daughters. His second marriage was to a fellow police officer, Heather King, and he adopted her son from a previous relationship.

For the next few years, Mallett ran patrol units and bicycle units and oversaw field training for new officers. He returned to the investigations unit in 2003, which was the same year Heather gave birth to their daughter, Maegan. In 2005, Mallet was promoted to sergeant and led a patrol unit for three years before returning for a third stretch in investigations in 2008, where he ran into a case that entangled his personal and professional lives in ways he could have never imagined.

❁ ❁ ❁

In the fall of 2009, Samira Watkins was a 25-year-old single mother studying to be a dental assistant while balancing a full-time job as manager of a McDonald's on the west side of Pensacola.

After Samira finished her shift at McDonald's on Thursday, October 29, around 8:30 p.m., she dropped her 4-year-old son off with her grandmother and told her family she was going to see her new boyfriend, Ricky, at his apartment and probably wouldn't be back until the next morning. After not hearing from Samira for two days, her family went to the Pensacola police and filed a missing person report. They also told police Samira was two months pregnant with Ricky's child, although the family had yet to meet him in person. According to her sister, Samira went over to Ricky's apartment that night to discuss the pregnancy. Once Samira's disappearance hit the news, the public outcry was swift as the idea of a young, pregnant mother disappearing shook the community to its core.

Of all the people Samira worked with during her time as a manager at McDonald's, one of the people she was closest to was Mallett's mother, Akiko, who worked there part-time. She added to a growing chorus of people in the community clamoring for answers on what happened to the young mother. Mallett was quickly inserted to oversee the investigation.

"You have to solve this case," Akiko pleaded with her son. "You have to find out what happened to Samira."

Five days after Samira went missing, two men boating in one of Pensacola's bayous saw a gigantic duffel bag floating in the water and when they got closer, they could see padlocks fastened over the zippers. When one of them reached down to touch the bag, they said it felt like there was a human body inside. When the police took the bag out of the water and opened it, they found Samira's body crammed inside, naked except for a red bra. Her head was wrapped in several layers of duct tape, from her chin to her forehead, and the condition of her body was such that the Medical Examiner couldn't tell whether she'd still been alive when she was placed in the bag.

By the time Samira's body was found, Mallett and lead detective Jon Thacker knew Samira's boyfriend's real name wasn't Ricky. His real name was Zack Littleton, and he was a married, 26-year-old Navy officer stationed at Naval Air Station (NAS) Pensacola who was in the process of moving out of the apartment Samira visited because his wife, who was also in the military, was moving to Pensacola from South Carolina with their infant child and the family was moving into a rental home.

According to her family, Samira and Littleton met at a nightclub in Pensacola that summer and dated for two months before she found out she was pregnant. When she told Littleton about the pregnancy, he'd become upset and tried to talk her into getting an abortion. Samira refused and told him she hoped she could count on him for support. When Littleton first spoke with police, he said he was just friends with Samira until finally admitting the two had a sexual relationship.

The night Samira went missing, one of Littleton's neighbors saw her arguing with him outside of his apartment. The neighbor said Littleton was acting "aggressive" toward Samira as they stood in front of her red Ford Taurus until she calmed him down and they went inside his apartment. The Taurus still hadn't been found, and as the investigative team put together the timeline of Samira's final hours, they kept coming back to the missing car. The team felt it was essential to unlocking the case, although not just necessarily by finding it, which the police did a few days later, abandoned on the opposite side of town from the bayou where her body was discovered.

"So if he moves the car, how does he get back home?" Mallett asked. "Either he has to involve somebody else, like a friend, or just somebody to give him a ride in some other mode of transportation."

In an era where ride-sharing apps like Uber and Lyft were only in big cities and hadn't reached Pensacola yet, the team pulled logbooks from every taxi company in the area for the nights surrounding Samira's disappearance, even if they didn't know exactly what they were looking for right away. One of the detectives on the case, Shannan Briarton, began poring over the logbooks. While working another off-duty job, Briarton would give the logbooks another read. The third or fourth time through, she found something. It was an entry for a pickup of "Zack" at a Waffle House in Pensacola in the early morning hours of October 30 and just two blocks from where police found Samira's car. The drop-off location was just blocks from the rental home Littleton was preparing to move to with his family.

In a video that police obtained from Waffle House, Littleton walks into the restaurant and asks if he can use the phone while carrying a container of Clorox wipes. The police obtained a search warrant for the rental home Littleton was preparing to move his family to, where they found a gold earring that matched the one taken from Samira's body and paper towels with the same floral imprint as the ones found in the duffel bag with her body.

Littleton's computer revealed Google searches in the days leading up to Samira's murder that seemed to incriminate him:

- *Abortion clinics in Pensacola*
- *Effects of sulfur on human remains*
- *What lyme does to dead bodies*
- *Bodies in landfills*
- *How to speed up decomposition of a human body*

Littleton was arrested on November 23, 2009. Thacker called Samira's family to tell them the news. Mallett called his mother to tell her.

On June 30, 2011, Littleton was convicted of first-degree murder and sentenced to life in prison without the possibility of parole. He showed no emotion as the verdict was read. Littleton's wife, who was sitting in the back of the courtroom, got up and walked out of the courtroom during the reading of the verdict. Samira's family, sitting just three rows back from Littleton, grasped each other's hands and wept.

✿ ✿ ✿

Mallett's promotion to lieutenant made the front page of the *Pensac-ola News Journal* on November 17, 2012, with a picture of a smiling Mallett, now 44 years old, as he received his lieutenant's pin from his 9-year-old daughter, Maegan.

After his promotion to lieutenant, Mallett oversaw the patrol division's day shift for six months before moving back to investigations. In 2016, Mallett's 26th year with the department, he was promoted to captain. In January 2019, he took over as the head of the entire Criminal Investigations Division, where the department's most important cases — crimes against persons — all landed.

It was an opportunity Mallett was determined to not let go to waste.

15

THE CIVILIAN

It was a stroke of luck the careers of Carolynn Stephens and Nicole Heintzelman overlapped the way they did at the Pensacola Police Department. The two represented a succession of brilliant, female forensic analysts working in the same department for five consecutive decades that came to represent an advantage against criminals that, in most cases, couldn't be overcome because they were both so good at their jobs.

Stephens worked on Tonya's case from the day her body was found in 1985 through her retirement in 2010 — the entire length of her career minus six months. She kept the search for the killer going over the years by reaching out to the FBI for forensic help in the pre-DNA era and then initiating new rounds of DNA testing as technology advanced. When she retired, Stephens called Tonya's unsolved murder her "white whale" — the term outgoing cops used to refer to the cases they knew would continue to haunt them after their careers were over.

Heintzelman, like Stephens, had finished at the top of her police academy class and, like Stephens, didn't have a direct path to working for the PPD. Her first job in law enforcement was as a crime scene technician at the Santa Rosa County Sheriff's Office in the late 1990s.

Unlike Pensacola, the forensics jobs in Santa Rosa County were considered civilian employees, which Heintzelman quickly discovered was code for low pay, no pension and no benefits.

When she worked for Santa Rosa County, one of the things Heintzelman enjoyed the most was attending monthly meetings of crime scene analysts from the different law enforcement bureaus in Florida's panhandle to go over crime scenes, share new techniques and run ideas past each other. It was obvious to Heintzelman the analysts from Pensacola always seemed to be ahead of the curve, which she deduced had a lot to do with the fact they were sworn officers and not civilian employees. Heintzelman impressed enough people in her role in Santa Rosa County that she was hired on as a full-time crime scene analyst by the PPD in 2001.

Unlike Stephens and Grant, Heintzelman spent her entire career using DNA as a viable crime-solving technique, and in 2015, she worked directly with Paul Kelly as he traveled to Jacksonville to try to track down a familial DNA match in Tonya's case tied to a convicted felon. While Heintzelman helped Kelly clear a half-dozen suspects through DNA testing in Jacksonville, it hadn't resulted in any arrests. Still, the new technology made a lasting impression on Heintzelman. Enough so that she began to wonder, like so many in her field did, what the future might hold.

* * *

On April 25, 2018, Joseph James DeAngelo, a 72-year-old retired police officer and truck mechanic living in Sacramento, California, was taken into custody and revealed as the individual behind at least 13 murders, 51 rapes and 123 home invasions in California from 1974 to 1986. DeAngelo's crimes spanned the entire state, and he was known at different times before his capture as the Visalia Ransacker, East Area Rapist, Original Night Stalker and the Golden State Killer.

DeAngelo was caught using a groundbreaking technique in which DNA taken from the scenes of the crimes was uploaded to a free genealogy website, GEDMatch.com, where several of DeAngelo's distant relatives had uploaded their DNA. The names from those matches — in this case, second cousins of DeAngelo — were used to reverse-engineer a family tree using obituaries, birth notices and voluntary DNA samples until it led police to DeAngelo's door. It was a game-changing leap forward in using DNA to solve crimes following the familial DNA breakthroughs in the mid-2010s.

In August 2020, DeAngelo pleaded guilty to first-degree murder and kidnapping and was sentenced to life in prison without the possibility of parole. DeAngelo's plea agreement spared him the death penalty but required him to admit to crimes he couldn't be charged with because of the statute of limitations, including dozens of rapes and home invasions.

Heintzelman threw herself into learning the ins and outs of the new "genetic genealogy" method used to catch DeAngelo with the thought of eventually using it to solve one of Pensacola's most infamous unsolved cases — the disappearance of 25-year-old Tiffany Daniels.

Daniels disappeared after leaving her job as a theater technician at Pensacola State College — formerly known as Pensacola Junior College — shortly before 5 p.m. on August 12, 2013. She was already scheduled to take time off from work, so she wasn't reported missing for several days, and it wasn't until eight days after she was last seen in Pensacola that her Toyota 4Runner was found abandoned in a parking lot on the west end of Pensacola Beach, close to the entrance to the Fort Pickens campground. Daniels' vehicle was unlocked, and all of her belongings were still inside.

The review of security cameras on Pensacola Beach showed Daniels' vehicle going through the toll booth to the beach several hours after she left work, although residents in the area said the car had only been in the parking lot for a few days, and the cameras didn't give a clear image of who was driving her car when it went through the toll booth. Throwing more confusion into the mix, Daniels' roommate claimed he heard her leave their home early on the morning of August 13.

To begin with, the investigation into Daniels' disappearance was a joint effort between the Escambia County Sheriff's Office and the Pensacola police, but the case ultimately landed with the PPD because she was last seen in Pensacola city limits. Over the years, lead after lead resulted in dead ends while Daniels remained missing. The best guess from the police was she'd drowned while swimming in the

Gulf of Mexico. Daniels' family believed she'd been kidnapped and murdered or even possibly sex trafficked and was still alive and being held somewhere.

Daniels' vehicle, which remained in the PPD impound lot for over a decade, produced two unidentified touch DNA samples, so Heintzelman reached out to Parabon Nanolabs, a company in Virginia specializing in genealogical investigations. In Parabon's presentation to the Pensacola police, they went over how they ran a case from start to finish but made it clear they couldn't use its resources on the Daniels case. Parabon's policy at the time dictated that only homicides, sexual assaults and unidentified remains were eligible for their services. With Daniels no longer a possibility, Heintzelman's mind immediately went to the unsolved rape and murder of Tonya Ethridge McKinley, where she knew there was plenty of physical evidence left to take DNA samples from. Initially, Heintzelman approached the head of the Criminal Investigations Division, Kristin Brown, at the end of 2018 about sending DNA from Tonya's case to the Florida Department of Law Enforcement but incorrectly sent the control sample — not the DNA extract — and by the time she got back around to sending it again, Mallett had taken over for Brown as the head of CID.

Like Heintzelman, Mallett followed the Golden State Killer arrest in California and was intrigued by how genetic genealogy testing might work for a Pensacola cold case. He already had a working knowledge of Tonya's case after helping Paul Kelly with his investigation in 2009, so after Mallett took over CID, and with the blessing of PPD Chief Tommi Lyter, the two began taking the first steps toward reopening the investigation into Tonya's murder.

✿ ✿ ✿

Within weeks, Heintzelman received an email from FDLE Chief of Forensic Services Lori Napolitano to inform her the state was going to pay $5,000 for one round of Parabon's testing for Tonya's case. This replaced the $5,000 already committed on behalf of the PPD. After a further review of the genetic evidence still available in Tonya's case, all agreed the evidence had been so expertly preserved over the years that it met or exceeded every parameter Parabon needed to begin testing.

"When we talk about cold cases in our department, for the last 34 years this case had been at the forefront of our minds," Mallett said. "I'd worked on it in the past. I was very interested in it, to say the least."

It was the first time a law enforcement agency in Northwest Florida would attempt to solve a case using the genetic genealogy method and, from what anyone could tell, only the second time in Florida. The first step was having Parabon produce a phenotype for the DNA, which identified the race, hair color and eye color of the killer. In February 2019, Mallett received the phenotype results — Tonya's killer was a white male with light brown or sandy blond hair and green eyes.

※ ※ ※

One moment police wished they could have back from the early days of the investigation was when they told Tonya's family she hadn't been sexually assaulted before she was murdered. For decades, Tonya's family believed the only possibility of DNA evidence in the case, if it existed, came from underneath Tonya's fingernails as she'd fought off her killer. But this was only a guess derived from the state of her body following her death. Part of Mallett's approach in 2019 was to walk that back if he had the chance.

"Saying she wasn't raped was a mistake," Mallett said. "There were some of us who believed she was raped [in 1985], and all of us believe that now."

Tim Davidson was no longer considered a suspect because he'd been cleared through DNA testing multiple times. The retired detectives who worked the case, whom Mallett lovingly referred to as the "old-timers," were all still convinced Kurt Lisk was the killer despite his having been cleared through DNA testing three times.

Mallett was determined to keep knowledge of the investigation to a close circle. He didn't want Tonya's family and friends to know, so they wouldn't get their hopes up and because some of them could still be suspects. For Mallett, the clearest path to solving the case was through science and secrecy. Nothing would be done in the traditional sense.

"We're going to understand the case and all the details, but it's not something we're going back into in that regard, as far as going out and interviewing people again," Mallett said. "That's been done. This is about science and finding out what we can from the DNA evidence."

On May 24, 2019, Mallett held a meeting in his office with three detectives from the investigations unit to bring them up to speed — Marcus Savage, Adam McCoy and Jon Thacker — who'd teamed up with Mallett to help solve the Samira Watkins case in 2009. The group went over details about Tonya's family, reviewed old suspects, and Mallett explained the basic science of how the genetic genealogy DNA technique was used. Specifically, he talked about the importance of centimorgans, which is the metric used for DNA testing.

If a person uploaded their DNA into a genealogy website where both of their parents already had their individual DNA on the same website anonymously, each of the parents would come back as a match of approximately 3,500 centimorgans to their child's DNA sample. This was exactly half of the 7,000 centimorgans in a single DNA sample. For first cousins, a match registered around 1,000 to 1,500 centimorgans. In Tonya's case, the hope was to find a match for a second or third cousin which would register around 150 centimorgans.

With the first round of testing underway, Parabon already had an idea of the scope of work needed to bring a resolution to the case. Parabon used a scale of 1 to 5 to assess investigations, with 1 being an absolute certainty the case could be solved and 5 being an absolute certainty it could not. Parabon told Mallett they labeled Tonya's case as a 4 on that scale, meaning the most likely outcome was the case couldn't be solved.

"It's not great news right off the bat," Mallett told his detectives. "But we don't go for the easy shit. We're fine with things being hard."

Mallett received the results from Parabon's first round of tests at the beginning of June, and it included seven names obtained through comparisons from the open-source genealogy website GEDMatch.com. Centimorgan levels indicated all were presumably distant third cousins of the suspect, and out of those seven matches, Parabon described three of them as "good" because they had ties to northern Florida and southern Alabama. The next step was finding out as much information as possible about the people behind the matches, which meant vetting them to figure out the best candidates to approach for obtaining DNA samples that might fill out the family trees. Mallett made sure to let everyone know to protect the identities of people whose names came up in the Parabon results, who he felt were equivalent to innocent bystanders.

Throughout the first part of 2019, several lawsuits filed against genealogy-based websites moved forward, including one against GEDMatch.com, which Parabon and the state of Florida were using for their genetic genealogy investigations. The gist of the lawsuits was that the fine print that people signed before submitting DNA samples online didn't make it clear their genetic material could be used for other purposes, like police investigations, and therefore violated their Fourth Amendment rights as a version of illegal search and seizure. In Tonya's investigation, the DNA evidence sent to Parabon proved to be an unwitting buzzer-beater. It was the last investigation in Florida with access to GEDMatch.com's stockpile of over 1 million samples in its database. Moving forward, because of the lawsuits, the number of accessible DNA samples for investigations like Tonya's case was reduced to approximately 300,000.

PPD crime data analyst Carolyn Connors was the point person for vetting potential witnesses and suspects from Parabon's list by scouring whatever information was available on the internet, which for most people usually meant almost everything about them. Connors worked quickly and efficiently and provided background dossiers to Mallett on all seven people within days. On June 19, 2019, Mallett convened the first meeting of his secret task force investigating Tonya's case.

The meeting was held in the Major Cases Room, which was lined with whiteboards that were specially fitted with drop-down curtains to protect the information from ongoing investigations that was on the boards. In the middle of the room was a gigantic wooden table taken from the old Pensacola police station with badges from retired officers sunk and lacquered into each corner. At the front of the room was an oversized digital screen for video presentations. Among those in attendance at that first meeting were Mallett, Heintzelman (forensics), Adam McCoy (investigations), Jon Thacker (investigations), and Carolyn Connors (online forensics). FDLE Forensics Chief Lori Napolitano joined via a digital link on the main screen.

Mallett wasn't above a good dad joke and opened things by giving the group a corny nickname — "The Gene Team" — which was met with several knowing groans before he dove into strategy. The initial thrust of the case was Connors vetting names from Parabon to turn over to Mallett, who had to decide whom to approach for DNA samples to fill out family trees. Mallett had one very specific rule, which was that no one in Pensacola or the surrounding area could be approached for samples to begin with. This fell in line with his need to keep the investigation secret for as long as he could, and he reassured the group that Connors already had a few promising leads from outside of the area.

Mallett closed the meeting with good news. Because of the pending lawsuits against GEDMatch.com, the FDLE decided it wasn't going to open any new cases using the genetic genealogy method in 2019, which meant an extra $5,000 earmarked by the FDLE for a different investigation was going to be applied to Tonya's investigation. This meant there would be three rounds of testing, with two paid for by the FDLE and one paid for by the PPD at a total cost of $15,000.

Mallett and his wife Heather were scheduled to take their youngest daughter Maegan to band camp at Florida State in a few weeks, and there were a few matches around Tallahassee who might be good candidates to ask for samples. Mallett planned to contact them ahead of time via phone and meet with them to obtain DNA if they were willing. Another promising connection to the case was in Texas, which Mallett said would require him or someone else from the department to travel. Because both the original case file and the first round of Parabon results had several connections to Texas, this was deemed a priority.

The last of Mallett's directives seemed to straddle both the legal and ethical gray area of the case. Legally, the police were allowed to concoct stories to obtain DNA samples. This just meant they could lie if they wanted to, but Mallett didn't want to go that route.

"I want to reemphasize we are going to be very, very careful with everyone we talk to or approach in this case," Mallett said. "But I've thought this over, and we need to be up-front with everyone we approach. My worry is if word gets around that we're using this way of solving cases through genetic genealogy and we're trying to trick people into helping us, it might hurt a cop in the future who is going to get a sample or wants to solve a case like this. So we'll be really careful about who we talk to ... but whoever we do talk with we're going to tell them the truth about why we're there."

The group spent the rest of the time talking about the unknown suspect. They agreed the target age was someone born between 1960 and 1965, which would have put him in his early 20s in 1984 and 1985. There was also a short discussion on obtaining ancestry kits to give out to people for DNA samples, and some expressed sticker shock in the room after discovering each kit cost $200. Mallett ended the meeting with a warning.

"If you do find yourself face-to-face with a suspect, be careful," he told the group. "We all know what he's capable of."

Carolyn Connors identified a woman in Texas as a distant match to the suspect's DNA sample and thought she might be willing to help out because her social media featured several pro-police posts. Connors' instincts were right. Mallett spoke with the woman on the phone, and she agreed to not only send a DNA sample to Pensacola but also volunteered to pay the $200 for the sample kit.

On July 5, 2019, Mallett emailed the group to say he made contact with a man from the Parabon list who lived outside of Tallahassee, and he'd agreed to submit a DNA sample as well.

Mallett called another meeting on August 16, 2019, to introduce two new members of the task force, Danny Harnett and Kevin Christman, and bring them up to speed. Harnett was a veteran detective who had worked closely with Mallett for years and was making his return to investigations. Harnett, like Mallett, had gone through a nasty divorce and sought out a promotion from detective to sergeant once his daughters were old enough for him to work 12-hour patrol shifts, which was required of the promotion. When a detective sergeant spot came open under Mallett in investigations, he was brought back into the fold and pulled directly into Tonya's case.

At the same time, Christman was in the process of taking over the investigations division from Mallett, who was now in an all-encompassing administrative role within the police department. The new role allowed him to serve as the unofficial interim police chief while Tommi Lyter, who'd been chief since 2017, was away on personal leave to care for his wife, who was dying from cancer.

Mallett trusted Harnett and Christman as much as anyone he'd ever worked with, and while Christman was going to be mostly hands-off unless called upon, Harnett's role was akin to an elite defensive player in the NBA who gets traded from a shitty team to a team with a shot at winning the championship in the middle of the season. His total focus was on how he could help the team win it all and he was willing to do that by any means necessary.

"When I started as a cop, this was a case the old-timers would bring up again from time to time because it was such unusual circumstances," Harnett said. "When I came back to investigations and heard about the DNA stuff and the centimorgans, that was kind of Greek to me, but I tried my best to understand it. I'm more like ... give me a target and give me something to go at. I think that's where I'm at my best."

In October, Mallett sent the additional DNA samples to Parabon for the second round of testing as he continued to work plotting out family trees, which was the most painstaking and time-consuming part of the investigation. The most complicated parts of the investigation seemed to come naturally for Mallett, including his understanding of the science and the methods behind its practical applications. Early on, he took over a small office next to his and had four gigantic whiteboards installed — one on each wall — where he mapped out family trees tied to the killer's DNA. After six months of work, his research on the family trees now stretched back to the mid-1800s. Mallett's youngest daughter, Maegan, was a junior in high school, and with both parents working at the police station, she found herself helping her father with his project on some days after school. Maegan's section of the whiteboards used purple, green and pink dry-erase pens in blocks of text that were sideways in some places and diagonal in others. Mallett's sections were all perfectly squared, perfectly written blocks of text, all with the same black pens. The contrast between the two different types of handwriting — and the fact of who the handwriting belonged to — along with the mapping of family trees served as a stark reminder of the humanity that continued to propel the case forward.

"He's somewhere in there," Mallett said, gesturing at the whiteboards as his daughter worked behind him. "We think. We hope."

✿ ✿ ✿

If there was a low point in the investigation, it probably came in November 2019 after the results from Parabon's second round of testing came back. Mallett summoned the task force for a meeting a few days before Thanksgiving to go over the results, which did a considerable amount to expand family trees but also added an unexpected layer of confusion.

The two most promising family trees showed extensive ties to southern Alabama and northern Florida, which was good news because it meant the killer was almost certainly local. The confusion occurred when a representative from Parabon attending the meeting via digital link said a "massive amount of pedigree collapse" was detected between the two family trees, which made it difficult to identify specific lineages. The members of the task force exchanged confused glances. Someone in the room asked what pedigree collapse meant.

"Pedigree collapse is what happens when two individuals who share an ancestor reproduce," said the Parabon rep. "It makes the number of distinct, unique ancestors in a single family tree difficult to identify. It's more commonly known as inbreeding ... it makes it harder to identify the suspect."

"That's fucked up," Harnett said under his breath.

Parabon produced seven new names from the second round of testing that it believed could clear up some of the confusion around the pedigree collapse/inbreeding by obtaining extra DNA samples, but all of the candidates were located in the Pensacola area. Which meant they were off-limits, per Mallett's rule.

In the early stages of the investigation, Mallett made sure to temper initial optimism with hard facts to keep everyone grounded. He wanted to make it clear there was no rabbit to pull out of a hat. Now, sensing a shift in the room, he decided to send the investigation in a new direction. He instructed Connors to begin vetting people with ties to the Pensacola area about DNA samples. This included a handful of people from Tonya's hometown of Milton.

"Look at it this way," Mallett said. "This just means if we find a suspect who has connections to two of these family trees, it's either a great, amazing lead and we're not far off or it has a good chance of actually being our suspect. And if people start to find out what we've been doing, that's fine. People do crazy things when they start thinking they're under that type of pressure, so who knows?"

Working off Connors' vetting of DNA sample candidates, Mallett made contact with five of the seven people from Parabon's list and was able to obtain DNA samples from three of them. Through his work on the whiteboards, Mallett added two more names to the list and obtained a total of five new samples for the final round of DNA testing. Around this same time, the FDLE reached out to Mallett and told him after completing work on another case they could lend more resources to Tonya's investigation moving forward. This meant FDLE agents and, hopefully, a mobile DNA testing unit would be in Pensacola for the rest of the investigation. On December 17, 2019, Mallett emailed the task force to say he was finished with most of the work on Parabon's to-do list and they would all reconvene early in the new year.

"Lori [Napolitano] and the FDLE are doing a great job and bringing us leads," Mallett wrote. "I will let you know when one of them allows us to narrow our focus."

16

ENDGAME

On Monday, February 10, 2020, the Florida Department of Law Enforcement and the Pensacola Police Department identified a suspect in the murder of Tonya Ethridge McKinley. It was just a few weeks past what would have been her 59th birthday and 36 years after her body was found on January 1, 1985 in an upper-middle-class neighborhood just off Escambia Bay.

The name of the suspect was Daniel Leonard Wells, a 57-year-old professional woodworker who lived in Pensacola but grew up in Milton, just like Tonya. Mallett's initial guess on the suspect's age was someone born between 1960 and 1965. Wells was born in 1962, so he would have been 22 years old in 1984.

Wells had several arrests on his record in Pensacola in the years immediately following Tonya's murder. In 1987 he was arrested for battery and for tampering with a witness. In 1989 he was arrested for solicitation of prostitution. There were property records for Wells and his family dating back decades in the Pensacola area, and he was listed as the current owner of a home on Cerny Street in Pensacola. One of Wells' older sisters, Nan Wells, owned a home on the same street.

Mallett spent most of that first morning doing covert surveillance on Wells. He followed him from his home to his job and back again, clocking the stops he made during the day to get a feel for his routine. While Mallett tracked Wells in real life, Connors tracked Wells online. By the end of the day, they began to get a more complete picture of Wells' life and crimes.

❋ ❋

Sometime in the early 1990s, Wells left Pensacola and moved to the Midwest, where he lived almost exclusively in the Kansas City area and didn't return to Florida until 2009. He was married and divorced twice and had a son from one of those marriages, Morgan, who was in his 20s and lived in Arizona.

While he was living in the Kansas City area, Wells was arrested for masturbating in public on one occasion, and on another occasion he was arrested for exposing himself to a woman. He was the subject of another half-dozen investigations where women chose not to press charges but accused him of the same things. In 1998, police arrested Wells for second-degree sexual assault in Missouri.

In one of the cases, Wells was standing by a dumpster like he was peeing and turned to expose himself. In another case that fit a pattern of incidents in the area, he was sitting in his truck in a parking lot at Walmart and asked a woman who walked by for directions. When she got close enough to his window, he moved the map he was holding over his lap to reveal he was masturbating.

Connors tracked down another compelling piece of evidence that first day, and one that seemed to tie Wells directly to the area in which Tonya's body was found. On a traffic ticket issued to Wells just a few months after Tonya's murder, he'd given police his address as a home on Elmcrest Street located about a mile from where Tonya's body was found.

The night Wells was identified, Mallett sent an email to the task force saying they would meet two days later, on Thursday.

"We have a suspect to look at," Mallett wrote. "This will catch everyone up and discuss the plan moving forward."

❋ ❋

Mallett started the Thursday meeting in the Major Cases Room by praising the FDLE for their work, then he launched into an explanation of how Wells was the first person to connect two of the family trees constructed via DNA testing. This was something else Mallett correctly predicted might happen after the now-infamous pedigree collapse/inbreeding meeting with Parabon in November.

Connors passed around an enlarged copy of Wells' driver's license, which was the first time most of the people in the room got to see him. Mallett shared the results of the phenotype report from February 2019 which said the subject likely had sandy blond or brown hair and green eyes. Wells' driver's license indicated he had green eyes and sandy blond hair.

"Well then," Heintzelman said, "that might be something."

The other thing that stood out about Wells was his size. He was listed on his driver's license at 6-foot-6 and 250 pounds, which made him bigger than almost everyone in the room except Adam McCoy, a 6-foot-4, 275-pound lieutenant detective who had fought in the Gulf War. Mallett told the group Wells sold a gun recently, and they were concerned he might arm himself or try to commit suicide if he sensed a confrontation with police was about to occur.

"If we have to go through a door, I'd like to be in on that," McCoy said.

"We could make that happen," Mallett said.

Harnett was assigned to take the lead on a surveillance team tasked with following Wells almost around the clock until an arrest was made. Using Google Maps, Harnett looked through Wells' neighborhood for places to park that wouldn't seem suspicious to anyone who regularly drove through the area. He also mapped out the neighborhood where Wells worked at CDC Woodworking, which was located in an area made up mostly of industrial buildings. In two days of surveillance, Mallett felt certain that almost without fail, Wells was someone who had the same routine every day of the week.

"He leaves his home about the same time every morning, gets to work about the same time, and leaves about the same time, give or take a few minutes," Mallett said. "Doesn't eat out, doesn't socialize outside of work. He stops at a Tom Thumb twice a day for cigarettes and coffee, but that's about it."

Next on the agenda was figuring out how to obtain a DNA sample from Wells without his knowledge, which was a tricky proposition. Someone suggested a trash rip, where trash left out on a curb by any individual was fair game and didn't require a search warrant. Heintzelman called the county trash collection service, pretended she was moving to Cerny Street, where Wells lived, and wanted to know what day trash was picked up. She was told it was picked up on Thursday mornings so any potential trash rip was at least a week away. The group agreed a better plan than a trash rip was to obtain a DNA sample through Harnett's surveillance. The hope here was Wells might discard something in public, which was most likely a cigarette butt, because he was a chain-smoker. If that sample matched the DNA from the crime scene, they could then obtain a search warrant for Wells' DNA. The search warrant meant police could go to his home to obtain a cheek swab and ask him to come in for an interview and if the DNA from the cheek swab matched the DNA from the crime scene, then they could get an arrest warrant.

DNA results usually took about six months to get back, but Mallett felt things might move quicker because the FDLE mobile DNA testing unit was in Pensacola and could have results within one week in some cases. Because it seemed like nothing in the case had worked like it was supposed to until this point, Mallett began to think things might start to swing his way. Either that or things were about to become so unpredictable that he could use it to his advantage.

By the final week of February, Harnett and two FDLE agents were following Wells almost around the clock. In an email sent to the task force on February 28, Mallett wrote that the extra manpower from FDLE pushed the investigation into "full-on mode," and Harnett's team was squarely focused on obtaining anything Wells might discard that contained his DNA.

＊＊＊

In over 20 years as a cop, Harnett had never been a part of an investigation like the one he now found himself in the middle of. While he had the utmost faith in Mallett, everything they'd done as they tried to find Tonya's killer ran contradictory to everything he'd learned about solving homicides. That wasn't to say he didn't believe in science or understand science being used in the case, which he did.

"What you really want to do," he said, "is catch a motherfucker red-handed."

For Harnett, everything was about the standard of proof.

"To me, Wells was just the name of some guy associated with a family tree," he said, "so I wasn't super confident just to, you know, be told this is the guy. That was until I started seeing his history, with the arrests in Missouri ... and it started to seem like he might fit the profile. Then it became interesting, because the thing that didn't make sense was that he'd been almost completely out of trouble for the last 20 years except for a traffic ticket. You think somebody who does this type of thing is going to screw up again, but his recent history didn't reflect that. Which was so curious to me, because in my experience, guys like this didn't just stop."

Harnett and the FDLE agents agreed that a discarded cigarette was going to be their best bet for getting a DNA sample, but Wells proved to be a frustrating subject.

"He didn't go and eat in restaurants, and when he did get lunch it was always take-out," Harnett said. "And the problem with the trash rip was we didn't know who was going in his house. We thought it was just him but that was much more difficult to prove ... we knew he had a relative who lived on the street. What we did know was that any time he was outside of work, he was smoking almost constantly."

There were several near misses when Wells was smoking outside of work but not directly in Harnett's line of sight. Several times, Harnett arrived just to see cigarette butts all over the ground. To secure a warrant, either Harnett or one of the FDLE agents had to physically see Wells drop the cigarette on the ground. One thing Harnett thought might work to his advantage was that Wells was, to put it lightly, a terrible driver. In the weeks they followed him, he sped everywhere he went, never seemed to use his turn signal and ran red lights and stop signs almost every time he drove. By March 4, Harnett was tired of playing the waiting game. He put together a plan to pull Wells over for any number of traffic violations on his way home from work. The gamble was that Wells would toss a cigarette from his window once he was pulled over, which was something he hadn't done for two weeks despite constantly smoking in his truck.

"So he leaves work and he's smoking right away, like usual," Harnett said. "Me and the FDLE agent are cutting through traffic like crazy, trying to get behind him and he's driving like a maniac and commits like three or four [moving] violations. My goal is to get behind him, but have the FDLE agent in the unmarked car right next to him so she can watch the cigarette butt go out the window."

With Wells sitting at a red light and blissfully unaware he was surrounded by cars full of FDLE agents, Harnett reached to hit the lights on his car to pull Wells over. At that same moment, a cigarette shot out of the truck window and onto the pavement in clear sight of both Harnett and the agents. As Wells sped off, the agents and Harnett turned their lights on and whipped their cars sideways to block traffic as Harnett got out and ran toward the discarded cigarette. It was an unbelievable break.

"It was a perfect situation," Harnett said. "He's smoking and he just dropped it perfectly out the window, right onto the ground and right in front of us."

Harnett brought the cigarette butt directly to Heintzelman, who had it in the possession of the FDLE and their mobile DNA testing unit within hours. The next day, the FDLE called Mallett to tell him the DNA from Wells' cigarette matched the DNA from the unknown subject in Tonya's case. Shortly after that, the state attorney's office called Mallett to tell him a search warrant for Wells' DNA wasn't going to be necessary because the DNA match from the cigarette was enough evidence to go directly to an arrest warrant.

Details of the charges were hashed out by the state attorney's office over the weekend. Mallett stayed mostly silent through the updates until the district attorney's office presented the two options they were looking at — first-degree murder and first-degree sexual battery or the lesser charge of second-degree murder. While Mallett believed the district attorney would do the right thing and go with the first-degree murder charge, he began to hedge his bets. Being charged with second-degree murder could mean Wells might be a free man again one day. This was a bridge too far for Mallett.

"I won't let it get to that," Mallett said. "I'll start calling in favors if I have to."

On Monday, March 16, the state attorney's office called Mallett to tell him they'd settled on charges that weren't presented to him initially. Wells would be charged with first-degree murder and first-degree sexual assault/rape, which gave prosecutors more leverage to seek the death penalty if they chose that route. On Tuesday, March 17, 2020 — St. Patrick's Day — Mallett met with a judge to go over the arrest warrant with a fine-tooth comb. In the warrant, Mallett gave a brief summation of Tonya's case leading up to the day Harnett and the FDLE agent recovered the cigarette they saw Wells toss from his truck.

"DNA was extracted from the cigarette butt and compared to DNA from the semen located at the scene of McKinley's murder," Mallett wrote. "The analysis revealed the DNA extracted from the cigarette butt matched the DNA from the semen found on McKinley's vaginal swab and found on the towel left by her body. The DNA profile is greater than 700 billion times more likely to occur if the sample originated from Daniel Wells than from an unrelated individual. Additional investigation revealed Wells listed an address on Elmcrest Drive on a traffic ticket in March 1985 — less than one mile from where McKinley was murdered.

"The numerous injuries on McKinley's body coupled with the partial removal of her pantyhose and the evidence of semen in her vagina and on the towel indicate McKinley was sexually battered just prior to or after her death. The evidence at the scene indicates that the person who left the semen in McKinley's vagina and on the towel left next to her body was involved in her sexual battery and murder and that person has been identified as Daniel Wells."

The judge thought the arrest warrant was unassailable. Mallett let the team know the arrest was going down the next day. That evening, to the surprise of everyone involved, Wells did something he hadn't done in over a month of being under surveillance.

On the last day he would likely ever spend as a free man, he went home early from work.

17

"A DEEP, DARK HOLE"

Mallett mostly stayed put in his office the morning of March 18 as various people associated with the case came and went. Around noon, his wife and his 16-year-old daughter Maegan brought him lunch. Heintzelman stopped in to tell Mallett the new machine used to take fingerprints digitally might not work with Wells because he was so tall. She suggested they do it the old way, which just involved rolling fingers across the ink and then across the paper.

"Commit a murder in the 1980s, get fingerprinted like it's the 1980s," Maegan said under her breath but still loud enough for Heintzelman and her father to hear her.

Heintzelman laughed. Mallett shook his head and looked at his daughter, incredulous.

"I worry sometimes," he said to her, "that maybe you've spent too much time around cops."

Shortly after 1 p.m., Mallett left the police station in an unmarked black Chevy SUV and drove to the neighborhood around where CDC Woodworking was located. He found an empty parking lot a few blocks away, while three unmarked cars with Pensacola police and Florida Department of Law Enforcement agents, including Harnett in a black Chevy Impala, patrolled the neighborhood and took up surveillance positions around Wells' workplace. There was also a marked patrol SUV with two detectives from the investigations team, Kelly Eierhart and Kylan Osley, in patrol uniforms. Back at the police station, two more officers were on standby and ready to roll at a moment's notice.

From where Mallett was parked he couldn't see the building Wells worked in but had a clear line of sight to Pace Boulevard. Wells turned left on Pace Boulevard every day after work to get to the Highway 90 exit about a half-mile away, and police planned to pull him over as soon as he made the turn. Mallett took calls from Heintzelman and Tommi Lyter, the chief of police, in quick succession before Harnett pulled up next to him in the Impala. The two made small talk from their cars for the better part of an hour as they waited.

"I want to write a fucking book when I retire," Harnett said at one point. "But not about any of this shit. Like a horror novel, maybe. It won't have cops in it."

At 3:12 p.m., Mallett's radio lit up. Wells was walking out of work and headed toward his truck. "Danny, you ready to roll out?" Mallett asked.

Harnett nodded, threw his car into gear and sped out of the parking lot toward Pace Boulevard. Mallett hung back until he saw Wells' red truck speeding down Pace Boulevard and the lights from the patrol SUV flashing behind him. The two detectives posing as patrol officers got Wells out of his truck under the pretense of COVID-19 precautions after Governor Ron DeSantis had closed down bars and restaurants around the state one day earlier. When Wells got out of his truck and turned around, he found Harnett staring back at him. Harnett introduced himself and told Wells he needed to come to the police station to talk with him "about a matter." It was a slight deviation from the original plan in that Harnett framed it like a command instead of a request.

"What's this about?" Wells asked.

"We can discuss that at the police station," Harnett said, gesturing toward the patrol SUV. "Right now we just need you to come with us."

Wells slowly walked toward the front of the SUV. At 6-foot-6, Wells towered over the officers who surrounded him. Harnett instructed

Wells to place his hands on the hood of the SUV. As one of the officers went to grab Wells' wrist, he jerked it away. A look of anger flashed across his face, and the two detectives moved, cat-quick, and shoved Wells face-first back onto the hood of the SUV. Just this slight display of force took the fight out of Wells, who was quickly handcuffed and placed in the back of the SUV. Mallett, who had been standing on the periphery, joined a procession of police vehicles with flashing lights as they sped back to the police station.

The police brought Wells in through a back entrance, up several flights of stairs, down a hallway and into a small interrogation room. They removed his handcuffs and left him by himself, with Wells completely unaware of the growing number of eyes within the station watching him. The room was sparse, and Wells sat at a small table with two empty chairs on each side of him. The only other objects in the room were a Bible and a pair of handcuffs attached to the table.

In the investigations unit, a large crowd gathered around a giant flat-screen television and waited for the interview to begin on a closed feed looped into the interrogation room. In Mallett's office, Maegan watched the same feed on the computer screen with her best friend, Taylor Miller.

After making Wells wait 30 minutes, Harnett walked in and sat directly to the right of Wells, directly between him and the door. Mallett put several file folders on the table and sat down to the left of Wells. Because of how tall he was, Wells' legs stretched out between the two detectives.

Mallett read Wells his rights, clarified he understood them and started the interview by asking Wells if he'd ever lived on Elmcrest Drive, specifically at the address just a half-mile from where Tonya's body was found. Wells said he never lived on Elmcrest. Mallett went into one of the folders and pulled out a copy of the speeding ticket Wells received for driving with a suspended license in March 1985.

On it, Wells listed his address as Elmcrest Drive. Lie No. 1.

☆ ☆ ☆

Mallett: I think we're going to end up jogging your memory about a lot of things as we go through this. You don't remember a lot of details except the really important stuff. I take that into account. It's been 35 years. It looks like [in 1985] you had a suspended driver's license. Maybe couldn't keep up with your insurance? Were there ever any other troubles back then? Anything with the Escambia County Sheriff's Office, like fighting? Maybe a battery charge?

Harnett: Ever been involved in a report? Maybe an arrest for battery that later on wasn't what it seemed?

Wells: Don't think so.

Mallet: Anything to do with prostitution? Soliciting a prostitute? You'd remember that.

Wells: I got pulled over one time. It wasn't for soliciting a prostitute. They went through my vehicle.

Mallett: No ticket? Not taken to jail?

Wells: No. Nothing like that

Mallett: Does it surprise you that I ran your record and you had both those arrests on there? For battery and for solicitation? You're older. You've got experience. Now I'm asking you questions so far that I already have the answers to. And you know you're not here because of anything that happened today. There's been work that's gone into this. Keep in mind there's a whole lot of work that's gone into this and remember that when I ask you something, it's better if the answers come from you. We're not here by accident.

Harnett: You don't remember being in handcuffs at all? Can you tell us about those times?

Wells: I guess it was the time in Brownsville?

Harnett: What happened then?

Wells: I guess we went downtown?

Harnett: They booked you. Took your picture. Arrests are certain things that cause trauma. People remember those things. It's not a normal everyday occurrence. So you do remember that day? Do you remember anything about the fight or a fight you had? Any other charges you can think of? Any other time in handcuffs?

Wells: (*Mumbles, shrugs his shoulders like he doesn't know*)

Harnett: We did run your history, so we know. Anything in Kansas City?

Wells: Lewd and lascivious act, I think.

Harnett: Was it just once?

Wells: Just once. And again in Liberty, one time. In Liberty, Missouri, that I exposed myself.

Harnett: What was going on in your life?

Wells: It was hard times. It was a divorce. Drinking and stuff, too, played a role in it.

Mallett: What happened during that incident?

Wells: I went to court. Did counseling for six months. That and probation.

Mallett: I mean the incident. Exposing yourself.

Wells: I was working at a friend's house. Peeing outside of a dumpster. Woman walked up to me. Made a comment to me. Said something to her rude. I was exposed. I wasn't masturbating or anything like that. That was the one outside of Liberty, Missouri.

Mallett: That was one incident. What was the other one?

Wells: I exposed myself to a lady in a parking lot. After I was drinking. I exposed myself. I was masturbating.

Mallett: Why would you do that?

Wells: I don't know.

Mallett: What about the other cases? Not the two you got arrested for. I know there were other cases. It's not just what you got caught for. When we contacted the police in Missouri they said it seemed similar to other cases — up to five — and those victims chose not to go forward.

Wells: That was Independence. Like 1992 through 1995 or something like that.

Mallett: Then again in 1998. What was going on that triggered you to behave like this? There was something going on.

Wells: Just drinking. Something with my childhood.

Harnett: When did you get divorced?

Wells: First time in 1998, I was married in 1990 or 1992 or 1993. I don't know.

Harnett: You weren't married before that?

Mallett: There was behavior prior to getting married. Marriage falls apart in 1998 so you go back to that behavior. Is that a fair statement?

Wells: Yeah, something like that. I was just being stupid. Don't know why.

Mallett: Dan ... I can't stress how important it is for where we're at now in this investigation for you to be truthful. I can't stress to you how important it is to be as truthful as you can right now. You say you're trying to remember but we're already having to spoon-feed you stuff.

Wells: I know. It's just embarrassing.

Harnett: There's nothing you can say that will embarrass us.

Mallett: I've been doing this for about 30 years ... [Harnett] has been doing it for something like 27 years ... we've investigated the worst of the worst. The worst crimes you can think of in Pensacola. So you can't hide behind embarrassment. It's time to come clean and be honest. That will get you through this. Be honest. When you exposed yourself, how did you get the girl to approach you?

Wells: I just pulled up to her in my truck.

Mallett: Why did she walk over?

Wells: I asked her for directions or something ... she walked over and she saw me.

Mallett: Law enforcement terms. From our point of view. You pulled up, saw a lady. You asked her for directions and lured her over to the truck and —

Wells: I was drinking. That was the only time I did that.

Mallett: OK. You're drinking. You lure her over to have her watch you masturbate. Why would you do that? Sexual arousal? Gratification? Was it the sexual part?

Wells: I would say that's right. The arousal.

Mallett: Did you use that story every time? That was the one you got arrested on, but there were other cases. Where were you by the dumpster?

Wells: That was Excelsior Springs.

Mallett: So what happened in Independence? That was another one where you exposed yourself and were masturbating.

Wells: Pulled into a parking lot, pulled up by somebody. Exposed myself. Gave me a thrill to show it to them and expose myself. As sick as it is.

Mallett: Like I said ... where we're at ... we've had plenty of people sit in that chair, some who did the wrong thing for the right reasons. They had family stuff happen to them. Most people are not cold-hearted and just like to hurt people. Some do, but there's a trigger. Some things contribute. Like you said with the alcohol and the family stuff, there's triggers. We understand the need ... that some guys need some kind of different stimulus. Doesn't mean they're a bad person. Just means they're a little different. What goes on behind closed doors ... can be a little bit freaky. We're not judging you. We don't think you're a bad person because of that.

Harnett: We're also not hanging your dirty laundry out for public consumption. It's just in this room. We're not trying to embarrass you. I do have kind of a question, I guess ... you look at what was happening in Missouri ... we look at the prostitution in Pensacola. Would you masturbate in front of them? Did you just have sex with them? What was it?

Wells: I never picked up a prostitute.

Mallett: So the first time you ever went out to get a prostitute in Pensacola it was when you got caught by the police?

Wells: I never ... I was going to a friend's house down on T Street, and they were just standing out there.

Harnett: There's a reason it happens. There are women standing out there because men will pay them money for sex. I'm just curious, here or Missouri, where you may have picked up prostitutes ... what the history is of you picking up prostitutes?

Wells: No. I've never picked up prostitutes. I would just ... some of them ... it was just ... the time in Kansas, the first time, I'm not even sure I talked to some of them. Because they had cameras.

Harnett: Was it by the dumpster?

Wells: No, that was coming back from work. Drinking beer and by an old hotel. She walked by the dumpster, she saw me, I exposed myself ... I wasn't trying to be lewd or anything. She called it in, and I got picked up for that. Shawnee, Kansas, that was a department store or something ... can't remember if I caught her attention but I got caught for that because there were cameras ... in Independence, I separated from my girlfriend I moved out there to be with, and we decided to go our separate ways.

Mallett: It's triggers. It's urges. How many times did you do it and not get their attention?

Wells: Maybe half a dozen times. Didn't do it very often. Didn't always get their attention.

Mallett: That's not that freaky. There's worse stuff we've seen. But to go back to the prostitution ... it doesn't really make sense to get caught the first time. Because of the money. Because they'll let you do whatever if you pay them. They'll let you get freaky.

Wells: That was the first time.

Mallett: You got caught the first time. OK.

Wells: I was just driving down the road. There were cops everywhere. Then they ransacked my truck.

Mallett: She wasn't in the car? Usually, they'll do those stings and tell you to go drive around the corner. Dress a female cop up like a prostitute.

Wells: I was just driving to see someone ... see a friend on T Street.

Mallett: Are you in a relationship now? When was last time?

Wells: Before I moved home in 2009. Not since I moved home.

Mallett: So you haven't acted like this since you came back to Pensacola? You're good with your life right now? Happy? What about alcohol consumption?

Wells: Alcohol ... no hard liquor. Just a few beers in the evening. No relationships since I moved back. Just working, working on my house. No relationships.

Mallett: OK. What about before 1990? When you were here. Before you moved to Missouri. You talked about homelife. Talked about your dad.

Wells: We come from a broken home. I had four older sisters. My dad and myself lived in Milton. Peggy was gone. Went to college. Sisters were older. Polly moved here. Nan went to college. Quincy went to girls school with her in Suwanee.

Mallett: How much older are your sisters?

Wells: Youngest is one year older. 63, 64, 65 ... Nan is 62 ... Polly is 65 ... I was born in 1962. Five years between us.

Mallett: Closest one to you is who? Quincy is two years older than you? How old when your parents got divorced?

Wells: I was about 13 years old. My mom was from Allentown, north of Milton. She moved outside of Atmore, then to Baton Rouge. She went back to school.

Mallett: Did the girls go with her?

Wells: No, she went by herself. Quincy went to girls school ... she was 13 or 14 ... then came back here and lived with my dad and myself. Went to Milton High.

Mallett: How is your relationship with your sisters?

Wells: Good now. Great back then.

Mallett: Weird you say it was so bad but it doesn't sound that bad.

Wells: Normal life. Growing up in Milton. Just normal.

Harnett: Unusual for a mom to just leave like that and not take kids. Were you mad at her? Did she find someone else?

Wells: She was with someone else. After that.

Harnett: I ask because I'm divorced and a dad. They live with me. They became angry at their mom over the years for whatever reason. You didn't feel that?

Wells: No. I was close to my mom. Not upset with my dad.

Mallett: There's gotta be something. When my ex left I got my two girls. Their mother had issues that didn't coincide with how I raised them ... was hard to reconcile that for the girls.

Wells: My mom drank, so that's where I got it from. Dad was totally sober.

Mallett: You graduated from Milton High in 1981 then moved over to Pensacola. We established that by 1985 ... you're over here by then, is that correct?

Wells: That's correct.

Mallett: So New Year's Eve 1984 to 1985, do you remember what you were doing that night?

Wells: No.

Mallett: What would you normally have done on New Year's Eve? If you went out, where would you go?

Wells: Go out to the beach. Go to some bars.

Harnett: What about Chan's? You go there?

Wells: Yeah after work we'd go there ... there was a disco out there by University Mall.

Mallett: You talking about Club 2001?

Wells: Yeah. 2001. Usually, I was out at the beach.

Mallett: There were three bars out by the mall.

Harnett: There was Chan's, Coconuts, Darryl's ... Bennigan's?

Wells: I don't remember Darryl's.

Mallett: What would you picture yourself doing back on New Year's Eve? Go out with friends?

Wells: Yeah I was out with a group. Never alone.

Mallett: What about Elmcrest? We mentioned that at the very beginning. Jog any memories?

Wells: I stayed with a John Pendergrast over on Bayou Texar. John and I were friends.

Harnett: When you were out on New Year's Eve when you were a young guy, were you looking for women or company? Ever get lucky?

Wells: Yeah, man. I got lucky.

Mallett: Were you averse to one-night stands? Most guys aren't. Meet a girl at the bar and they're willing ... you're not going to turn it down, right?

Wells: Yeah, I had a few one-night stands. Halloween I remember. That was out at the beach. Winter rates or whatever. A couple of friends get some rooms or whatever.

Mallett: But you don't remember Elmcrest? Still don't?

Wells: The address doesn't sound familiar. The name of the street yes. I rented a room ... John Pendergrast had a house ...

Mallett: (*Mallett takes out several pictures of Tonya dressed up to go out for New Year's Eve.*) This is what she would've looked like if she had gone out that night.

Wells: I don't know her. Never seen her. Never.

Mallett: Do you have any idea what we're talking about yet?

Wells: I don't. I don't have any idea what you're talking about.

Mallett: OK. Let's cut to the chase. That young lady I just showed you a picture of ... New Year's Eve 1984 going into 1985 ... early morning January 1, 1985 ... she was found dead on the side of the road. And I have the evidence that you're the one that was there.

Wells: No.

Mallett: I have irrefutable evidence that you were there. I'm not doing all of this on a guess. Or on a hunch. I'm telling you, you were there.

Wells: I wasn't there.

Mallett: You watch TV? Anything about crime?

Harnett: You know about DNA?

Wells: Mm-hm. (*Nodding yes*)

Mallett: Literally, 1 in 700 billion chances. You were there. That's where we're at, Dan. I'm not asking you.

Harnett: It's been 35 years. This is the first time you've talked about this to the police. We're sure of that. Have you noticed anything unusual in the last few weeks?

Mallett: Did you feel like someone was following you?

Wells: No.

Mallett: Well, we were.

Harnett: Your DNA was at this site. On this person.

Mallett: There is no other explanation. Your DNA is at this scene. It's nobody else's except yours. There's no other explanation.

Harnett: Again, this is your life. This is probably freaking you out a little bit. There's a story here, right? And you can choose to give us that story about what happened, the chain of events that led us to here. If you don't, it starts to look pretty bad as to why you're not explaining it.

Wells: I don't understand. I've never hurt anybody in my life. I mean, I've had one-night stands before —

Harnett: Never had a one-night stand with her?

Wells: No. I mean, you guys are going back to school days and stuff.

Harnett: Right now you're afraid if you had a one-night stand with her that we're going to find out that you're somehow responsible for her death. But we already know that you are.

Wells: There's no way, man.

Mallett: Just listen. It's been 35 years. It's been 35 years you haven't had to face this. One day you're at work. Everything's fine. You finish the day, and you're on your way home. One hour later we're telling you this. It's a shock. And totally normal human behavior to be defensive about it. Just like for a while, you didn't want to admit you exposed yourself and masturbated in front of women. Then it was "Whoops I was peeing then she said something then I said something" and then it turns out "Wait there was another time" ... we went through that whole process with you but we're starting it again and we're going to end up in the same place. I don't like playing games. We've been doing this too long. I'm going to give you the right information so you can tell your side of the story. But saying you're not there isn't going to work. The unknown is what precipitated it. What were the dynamics? What led to this result?

Wells: I wasn't there.

Mallett: The DNA proves it. Without a doubt.

Wells: It just blows me away ... I don't understand. I'm really confused.

Mallett: I'm a little bit confused too.

Wells: I don't know her. I've never hurt anybody.

Mallett: I can believe you don't know her. Maybe didn't know her beforehand. But you knew her that night. I'll paint a little of the picture for you. I said Elmcrest. I said 1985. Now why would you have given the police that as your address in 1985? The thing about Elmcrest and that address is that it was a half-mile away from where this happened. And I don't think that's a coincidence. And I'm telling you, just like I told you about Elmcrest, the DNA is proving you were there. And it's "I don't know" and "I don't remember" ... and that's not gonna work for you. The evidence we have at the scene paints a really ugly picture for you. It's not gentle. It wasn't an accident. If you let evidence tell the story, it paints a really ugly picture. This is your opportunity to soften that. We don't know the dynamics. We go into things with an open mind, because too often we go in thinking one thing and that's not it. But I'm going to be honest with you because that's all I can do with you. My profession forces me to be honest. The evidence tells me you were there. What it doesn't say is how everything happened. And then there's also the concern if there were the other things ... just like with "Oh wait, I masturbated once in front of someone ... then there was one more incident." This is your side of the story. It's all about you and getting this out. But I can't put words in your mouth. I can't tell you what to say. Only you can do that. But if you keep going with the lies and denials, like you have, it's only going to dig your hole deeper. But we'll call you on it. And every time you lie, we're gonna call you on it. Just like before. And about 45 minutes from now, you're gonna be sitting in that chair, and it's gonna feel like you're in a deep, dark hole, and you're gonna want to get out. And it might be too late. Don't dig that hole that deep. We're open, we're here to listen to your story. But you were there.

Wells: I just don't understand.

Mallett: Do you not believe me? Do you want to know how I know?

Harnett: Two weeks ago. You're driving on Palafox Avenue. Headed back to your shop. Do you remember behind you there were cop cars that all of a sudden were shutting off the street?

Wells: Yep.

Harnett: Do you remember what you did right before that? You threw a cigarette out your window. And I was in that police car.

Mallett: And there were two more FDLE agents.

Harnett: We picked up your cigarette. Your DNA matched the crime scene.

Wells: I'm just blown away. Maybe it was somebody ... maybe I had sex with somebody?

Harnett: There's a way to look at this, about certain things about your history. I'm sure you're blown away. We want your input. It's not difficult to come to a conclusion based on what we already have, with what we know happened with the prostitution thing and more specifically what we know happened in Missouri. So there, you pull up in a truck. You see an attractive woman. You call them over, and lure them if you will, to engage in a sexual act. It's not a leap to see what happened here. He lured them over to his vehicle. He engaged in a sexual act. Then he took them. OK? There are certain types of people that have done that in the past. They make movies about it. They write books about it. People will fantasize about what you did ... the notion of what you did. That's what Ted Bundy did. I'm not saying that you're Ted Bundy, but if you don't involve yourself in that process ... you understand what I'm saying? You've already lured women. Strangers. For your sexual gratification.

Wells: I've never forced sex on anybody.

Harnett: You've already lured women. Strange women. For your sexual gratification. And this one gets taken.

Wells: I never took anybody.

Harnett: New Year's Eve. 1985.

Mallett: Then explain to me, Dan, how your DNA ends up with this girl.

Wells: Unless I had sex with her, maybe, like a one-night stand, but after that ... don't have any recollection of anything.

Mallett: You lived in this area in that time.

Wells: I guess I did.

Mallett: This was a big deal back then. On the news.

Wells: I don't remember that.

Mallett: Then how does your DNA end up with her?

Wells: Unless I was with her I guess? Unless we had sex?

Mallett: I'm not asking you to theorize. I'm asking you to tell me.

Wells: Well, I guess I had sex with her or something. I don't remember her. I was with her I guess. I don't remember her. The name, the face ... I don't remember her. I guess if I was drinking and out partying it happened pretty regularly.

Mallett: How can your DNA ... significant events in your life, you remember. *Challenger* spacecraft, you remember when it blew up?

Wells: Yes.

Mallett: Me too. I can remember exactly where I was when it happened. So wouldn't you think, if you had sex with a girl, picked her up one night, then the next morning she's found dead ... don't you think that would be something you would remember? Then on the news, you find out she's dead. You'd remember that.

Wells: Yeah, you would.

Mallett: That's the most innocent scenario I can give you. Back then, were you drinking so much you can't —

Wells: No, I have a good memory.

Mallett: So the next day, her picture is in the paper, or two days later, and for you, it's "Oh my God, I just had sex with her on New Year's Eve." There's room there to mitigate some of that evidence. There's room there to make it look better than it does now.

Wells: It looks horrible.

Mallett: I can't fill in the blanks for you. I was a junior in high school. I was in Key West. I wasn't here ... you have to do that. You're the only one.

Harnett: Your son is in Arizona. He's 24 now. You stay in contact?

Wells: Yes. All the time.

Mallett: That's hard to do sometimes. I have a son. He's in the Air Force. He was in Japan for two years, now he's in Biloxi. That's only two hours down the road. We have a good relationship. Sometimes, though, we don't talk for two months and it's like "Hey, you're only two hours away, come on now ..." but you and Morgan have a good relationship?

Wells: Oh yeah. We do.

Mallett: He ever come to visit?

Wells: Yes.

Mallett: When's the last time?

Wells: About a year ago. He lives out there with his mom. They moved out there after —

Mallett: You don't have a good relationship with your sisters. Who do you have a relationship with?

Wells: My ex-wife. My second wife, Morgan's mom. I've always had a good relationship with her. She calls and checks on me sometimes.

Mallett: So what I don't think ... my only time knowing you is the last hour or so. I haven't known you before this. You don't seem like a cold-hearted person.

Wells: I'm not. I mean —

Mallett: It seems like you care what people think about you, to a certain extent. But your image to Morgan, especially, so what you do is important. Because you're a good father. So he grows up, and he's a better person than you are. My kids, I want them to be better than me. You seem like you want that for Morgan.

Wells: Yes.

Mallett: I'm telling you in the near future, if it comes out, without the details from you about what happened, it's going to be clear to Morgan that you're responsible. And without an explanation on how it got to that point, he's going to be left to fill in those blanks just like we are. Something happened out of the ordinary. I don't think this was ordinary. Something happened that night that let everything slide downhill. But you're the only one who can say it, Dan.

Wells: I can't. I'm right back where I was. I'm back where I started. I don't recognize her. I don't remember being with anybody on ... what was it ... New Year's Eve you said? I mean it very well could've happened. I could've had sex with her. But I was with several friends. We would go out and stuff like that ... there would be a group of us.

I remember being at the parking lot and you'd go out and have sex then go back in and go home a few hours later.

Mallett: That's right. Lots of dark corners. Like the University Mall parking lot ... people used that for sex all the time. Did you ever have sex there? Ever used that place to have sex?

Wells: No. Not there.

Mallett: But at the beach, you would?

Wells: Yeah, at the beach.

Harnett: Ever pick anybody up there? Or Chan's? Or Bennigan's?

Wells: No ... not that I can remember ... seriously I don't remember. I'm being totally honest with you.

Mallett: Well ... not really.

Harnett: Ehhh ... not really.

Mallett: You said you weren't doing stupid drinking back then. The heavy stupid drinking. You said you have a good memory. I can't believe you have a night where you have sex with a girl and the next day she winds up dead and you don't remember. You're not being honest. I can't believe a night you had sex with a girl and she ended up dead and you don't remember.

Wells: I don't remember ... I remember the story about her you told me.

Mallett: You have to remember. You were there. Your DNA was there. There's no saying you weren't there. I've seen the lab reports. Yours is 1 in 700 billion. It was you. You were there.

Harnett: Your DNA is on her. It's at the scene. So not only were you with her, you were there, too.

Mallett: I want to help you get through this. There's no avoiding it anymore ... 35 years and it is here, in front of you now.

Harnett: You've avoided this day for 35 years.

Mallett: There are two scenarios here. You have two options. Either you were always wondering when you were going to get that knock at your door, or you really didn't care. And I don't get the feeling that you don't care.

Wells: I'm a very caring person.

Harnett: The things you left at the scene back in 1985 ... people didn't think it would get them caught. But the last 25 years, with DNA, we can. There are facts here. You're not here accidentally. These facts have caught up with you ... you have a choice as to how this impacts you. Share your story about what led to this. If you don't paint the picture, you leave other people to do it for you. And that's not flattering. All they're gonna see is this single mother of an 18-month-old son that was murdered. And they're gonna see that you're responsible for it. How that happened and the chain of events that led to that ... if it's terrible, if it's you lured this girl and you knocked her out and you dragged her over here and you murdered her, then I can see why you don't want to say. Because that's terrible. But maybe something happened. Maybe you guys hit it off. Maybe your interaction with her was positive and maybe you're thinking ... this is someone I can have a relationship with ... then things go horribly, horribly wrong. Those two scenarios are different. The first guy is a monster. He needs to go away forever. We've been down this road before ... but it's never as simple as people want to sensationalize it to be. It never is. I've worked on 18 of these. Every story is different. Maybe 1 or 2 are monsters. The rest are regular people who got involved and caught up in bad situations that escalated and they didn't know what to do.

Mallett: We've sat in this room with monsters. We're not getting that feeling with you. We don't think you're a monster.

Wells: I'm not a monster ... I do know ... I was with her and stuff but I didn't give her a ride home. There was a group of us ... oh, God ... because I guess she lived over in Santa Rosa County or something. Bobby Hicks and a guy named Ralph James, they were with me. There was a group of people I went to school with me that were there. And ... we did have sex in the parking lot ... and other than that ... no, actually it was at the house. That's where, uh, John Pendergrast lived.

Harnett: Is that the house on Elmcrest?

Wells: I guess the house on Elmcrest. I don't recall the address, but I stayed there with them every now and then.

Harnett: Was [Pendergrast] out with you that night?

Wells: No. Those other guys were. They came by the house and they left with her.

Harnett: Well, tell us what happened.

Wells: I just ... I had sex with her ... I guess I met her at one of those bars. At University Mall. I don't know. It was one of those bars. It wasn't Chan's. I can't remember if it was one of those bars.

Harnett: Was it a restaurant?

Wells: I can't remember if it's a restaurant.

Mallett: Dan, be very careful. You're minimizing. You're doing a lot of "I guess" and "I think" but in reality, you know. I can already tell by the way you're acting you're relieved. Because it's been 35 years and you can finally get it off your chest. And it's hard. But you've gotta do it the right way. Which is ... because you remember the details. Tell us the details of what happened. Then we'll work through it with you.

Wells: It's been a while.

Harnett: Don't create details.

Wells: I'm not.

Mallett: It's still there. You don't have to go back and remember it. It's right there. You're looking for ways to soften it. I understand that. You're trying to look for the best way to present it.

Wells: It doesn't look great. It looks horrible.

Mallett: We recognize softening details. Telling your wife you were out late, that's a time to soften it up. This is not the time to do that. Because those details are very bright in your mind. This is a defining moment in your life.

Harnett: At some point, you've gotta stop lying. The monster keeps lying. You're gonna try and throw bullshit at us. It has to stop. We've been through this hundreds of times with people. This is your first time. We're at an advantage there. You have some ability to craft your outcome, but you have to explain your part in this. I don't care about what you've told us so far, let's get to what actually happened. We know what you're doing and what you're thinking. You have the ability to craft some of the outcome. If you're not that monster, tell us what happened.

Mallett: We ask questions we know the answers to. We have your DNA and we have other evidence. So when you tell your story and we can counter it with evidence, it reflects badly on you. When you're not honest, it reflects badly on you. And we'll call you out on it. The best thing to do is start at the beginning and tell the truth and exactly say what happened. Because every time you say "I guess" and "I think," it tells me that you're not being totally honest about that moment of the story. But there's no escape now except for the truth. So just start at the beginning.

Wells: OK. I remember her friend had left her. She wanted a ride home. We went by my house and we had a few drinks and stuff. It just ... it just escalated, from that. She um ... I just ... and it escalated. I think I hit her in the head and it knocked her out. And it was a traumatic blow and it killed her.

Harnett: What happened that made it get out of control?

Wells: I think we got into an argument over something ... I can't remember what it was. I don't know.

Mallett: Was it about having sex?

Wells: No. She was willing to. ... Ralph and those guys stopped by. Then they left.

Harnett: Did you have sex with her before?

Wells: We had consensual sex and stuff ... and then ...

Harnett: What happened to make things get out of hand?

Wells: I just ... it was ...

Mallett: Was it something she said? Can we be real here? Did she comment on your sexual performance? Did she want to leave, and you didn't want to leave yet?

Wells: No. Nothing on that. Something like that.

Mallett: Let's do something simple. You said you hit her in the head. What did you hit her in the head with?

Wells: I think it was a cutting board. A wooden block.

Harnett: Were other people there?

Wells: Bobby and Ralph came over while I was there. Then they left.

Mallett: Had you already had sex with her?

Wells: Yeah, once.

Mallett: Then they came over and hung out for a bit with y'all? Had drinks and then they left?

Wells: Then we got into a little bit of an argument and whatever from drinking and stuff ... it just kinda got out of hand. I was standing in the kitchen. She was standing there.

Harnett: You had sex in the bedroom once?

Wells: Yeah, well, uh ...

Mallett: You said once. So there was a second time? After you hit her?

Wells: Yes.

Mallett: You said that was a fatal blow. But she was just unconscious at least. So you had sex with her a second time.

Wells: Yes ... well ... I couldn't get her to respond. I couldn't believe what had happened.

Mallett: So what'd you do then?

Wells: I think I took her down the road. I took her down the road in my vehicle. I don't know what I was driving then. It may have been my truck.

Mallett: The truck you got the tickets in. Where'd you put her? In the truck?

Wells: In the passenger seat.

Harnett: Did she wake up at all?

Wells: No. I checked her pulse and all that stuff and just freaked out.

Harnett: Before or after you left her body? How did you eventually kill her?

Wells: I think it was strangulation. We were just getting into it. We got in a big fight.

Harnett: Where was she when you strangled her? Place you brought her or at the house?

Wells: At the house.

Mallett: What did you use?

Wells: Just my hands.

Harnett: So you had sex with her a second time? After she was hurt?

Wells: No ... well ... we thought we were gonna have sex again and we got into it. She slapped me. I was just pissed so I hit her with the cutting board.

Harnett: So the second time you would've had sex, she would've been unconscious. We have evidence that shows it. So she wouldn't have been a willing participant. Is that correct?

Wells: That's right. Well, she slapped me and then that second time I realized —

Mallett: Makes me think you wanted to have sex again and she didn't? Did the strangulation occur after the second time having sex or before? Hit her in the head, strangle her, have sex with her ... realize "Oh shit she's really hurt." Put her in the truck, drive her around, push her out on the side of road. Makes me think that the argument about having sex again ... that you hit her in the head and had sex with her. Did the strangulation occur after that or before?

Wells: Before.

Mallett: You're trying to have sex with her again and realize "Oh shit she's really hurt."

Wells: Yeah ... then I left her like a bag of trash. I'm um ... I can't believe it.

Mallett: Did she have other belongings with her? Purse? Shoes?

Wells: I'm sure.

Mallett: What'd you do with them?

Wells: I don't know what I did with them. I don't remember.

Harnett: When you had sex with her on Elmcrest the second time, was it in the kitchen where the cutting board was, or did you take her back in the bedroom?

Wells: Back in the bedroom. I think.

Mallett: What'd you do about the blood? In the house? I mean you cracked her in the head. Head wounds bleed.

Wells: I don't know. I just tried to clean it up.

Mallett: Where was Pendergrast? What time frame are we talking about now?

Wells: He was out for the night. Early morning. New Year's Eve, like you said.

Mallett: Where were you before that? Did you just show up by yourself?

Wells: I don't know. I was with a group of people.

Mallett: Who was with you?

Wells: Ralph James. Bobby Hicks. They were there.

Harnett: Both were there when you met this girl?

Wells: Yeah, both.

Mallett: You ever tell them what happened? They stopped by before the fight happened and they left? Did they ever say anything to you?

Wells: Never heard anything about it. Not that I know. Not from them.

Harnett: Then you see it in the paper. What's your life like in the months after that? You see it in the paper and think what? Ever want to tell anybody?

Wells: I was freaking out. It wasn't good. Yeah I did. Numerous times I did.

Harnett: Do you remember making a phone call or writing a letter about this? Somebody called and they were struggling ... they couldn't get it out. Write a letter to anybody?

Mallett: Did you ever tell anybody?

Wells: Nobody. Never. Just denial. Unbelievable. Sometimes I would think it was just like a dream. Because I would never hurt anybody. Never hurt anybody before, not even fighting in school. Came from growing up in a great background ... it's just not in my nature. It could've been cocaine. Those were cocaine days. The guys I rented the house from before turned me on to it. I knew it was bad. I did it off and on for maybe a couple of years. It alters ... everything. Alters your sex drive and everything.

Mallett: I can believe you're not normally an aggressive violent guy. I can't think of what she would've said or done. That's what I'm trying to figure out that set it off that night that evoked that response ... then to do the things you did afterward.

Wells: I was never aggressive. I just don't understand it. That's the truth. I hit her. I realized I hurt her bad. Then I just wanted it to be over with ... I just wanted it to be done. It was just that and cocaine. Straight sex.

Harnett: They found signs of anal sex in the autopsy. That's not what you were into?

Wells: I don't recall that.

Mallett: So what we're saying is you had sex with her. It was consensual. Then there was a fight. Was it a fight and a struggle? Then at the end of it, she's got several injuries. It doesn't indicate a quick argument. There's some indication it wasn't your hands. Hands leave a distinct mark.

Wells: I just remember hitting her over the head. It's been a long time. I don't know. Then the strangulation.

Mallett: There's an indication it wasn't your hands.

Wells: I've put it out of my mind ... maybe I used a belt or something. I don't know.

Mallett: Tell me what you know for sure. We're good at memory recall stuff.

Wells: I remember having sex with her. Doing a little more partying. Then getting into it for a bit. We got into an argument. She was ready to go. She wanted to leave. I was going to give her a ride to Avalon or wherever she lived. And she ... uh ... she didn't respond quick enough or whatever. I remember she hit me and I retaliated. I had that cutting board in my hand and hit her on top of her head.

Mallett: Then she went down on the ground and then you did ... you strangled her.

Harnett: Then you dragged her back and had sex with her.

Wells: I dragged her back down there ... I strangled her ... realized it was over.

Mallett: I might be able to fill in some blanks with you. I don't want to put words in your mouth. I'm going to tell you things that are known. See if it jogs your memory. Next to her body there's a towel. There's a bath towel. It's got her blood on it, and it's got DNA from you on it.

Wells: I don't remember.

Mallett: That comes from that house to being dropped off there with her.

Harnett: After you hit her on the head and strangle her you're gonna have blood on you, right? Do you remember cleaning up?

Wells: I'm sure I washed off.

Mallett: So you have this brief moment of rage. You're drinking and you're doing coke. You're not quite ready to go. You're having a high and you don't want to leave and she gets mad at you and slaps you. That kinda sets you off. Crack her in the head with the board. You realize you hurt her, so you strangle her. But you're still there and you start having sex with her again ... then you come back to reality and it's like "Oh, what have I done?" Did you try to give her any aid then? At any time?

Wells: Yeah I did. Right when I hit her and knocked her out. I checked her for breathing and this and that. I must have hit her hard. Then I strangled her.

Harnett: Well, you have to have known she was still alive. At some point, did she come to? Did she say anything?

Wells: No, she just ... she was like gurgling. I knew it was bad.

Mallett: Then you strangled her? Just to end it?

Wells: Yes.

Mallett: So you're out of your mind with rage? So you go from hitting her in the head to checking her to you need to end it so she doesn't tell on you. Then you decide to end it? You strangle her then take her to the bedroom to have sex with her? Then reality hits. The rage starts to fade and you get into —

Harnett: So you had consensual sex, then sex after she was unconscious, but not fully? Then you realize she's gone?

Mallett: Her purse and her shoes aren't at the scene.

Wells: I don't remember what I did with them. I have no idea.

Mallett: You're just freaked out.

Harnett: Well, we have the purse and shoes.

Mallett: Could you have thrown them out your truck window?

Wells: I could have. I don't know.

Mallett: See there are some things I can believe. Like after, you're not totally clear what happened with her stuff. That makes sense. But the moments of the fight, what happened right there, the act itself ... that's gonna be burned into your memory because it's such a significant event. So we know what we're talking about.

Harnett: Trauma in your life ... incidents and moments scar you and you don't forget them. I can tell you something that happened when I was five years old — that specific incident — but I can't tell you what happened around that. You'll know.

Mallett: I want to ask you something. Might seem inconsequential. An important piece of the puzzle to us. Did Pendergrast have pets?

Wells: Yes ... labs. Black labs.

Harnett: You talk to any of these guys after you come back to Pensacola?

Wells: No. I haven't seen anyone.

Mallett: So the only guys that saw you that night with her were Ralph James and Bobby Hicks. What about the bar?

Wells: If they remember.

Mallett: Well, let's just say they have great memories. What about the bar?

Wells: She wanted a ride home. Then she agreed to go by the house. Did some cocaine.

Harnett: Did she bring it or did you bring it?

Mallett: Did she use it?

Wells: Yeah. I think she did.

Mallett: Really? (*Note: Tests showed Tonya did not have cocaine in her system.*)

Wells: Well ... no she didn't. She had a few drinks.

Mallett: Drinks. Consensual sex. Two guys come over. They leave. She wants to go home.

Wells: That was getting into the early morning.

Mallett: The towel kind of bothers me. You would've obviously cleaned up. Cleaned up yourself. Your semen is in the towel, so you used it to clean yourself. Why take the towel with you?

Harnett: Did you put anything over her head when you hit her?

Wells: No. She was by the couch. I hit her, she fell to the floor, I took her to the bedroom.

Mallett: Did you maybe take the towel to keep blood from getting in your truck? I think that's the only part now that bothers me. The towel obviously came from there. When you dropped her on the side of the road ... how'd you do that?

Wells: Got there, put her on the side of the street. Took her out and set her down.

Mallett: Do you remember what that looked like? Do you remember what she was wearing that night?

Wells: No. I don't remember.

Mallett: You don't remember what she looked like when you left her on the side of the road?

Wells: I don't remember.

(*Mallett put crime scene photos of Tonya's dead body on the table in front of Wells.*)

Wells: I don't really wanna —

Mallett: That's how you left her. That's how. Is that consistent with what you remember?

Wells: I don't remember what she looked like. I just remember I took her out of the car.

Mallett: Just a girl you picked up in a bar.

Wells: Yes sir.

Mallett: Wrong night, wrong time.

Wells: Yes sir.

Harnett: You went to school together. You don't remember her.

Wells: I don't know her from high school. If she was older or what. Did not know her from school ... this is the first time I've seen her.

❖ ❖ ❖

After Wells confessed, Mallett went to his office and called Tim Davidson Jr. first, then Renee, to tell them an arrest had been made. Neither of them had any idea the investigation had even been reopened thanks to Mallett's veil of secrecy. Stunned, Tim Jr. began to cry, thanking Mallett over and over before he asked the name of the man they'd arrested. When Mallett told Renee about the arrest, she gasped audibly, then tried to talk but started to sob uncontrollably. At Mallett's invitation, both made plans to come to a press conference the next morning at the police station. After making the calls, Mallett and Harnett returned to the interrogation room, where Wells had been sitting in silence. Mallett and Harnett sat down with Wells and continued the interview.

❖ ❖ ❖

Mallett: I know something about you. I know you're not a monster.

Wells: This shouldn't have happened ... I shouldn't have continued on. We shoved each other. It's not my nature.

Mallet: For you, it's very emotional because we're bringing back a lot of stuff. It's difficult. Like we talked about a long time ago you did some coke ... stuff like that. The story came out in bits and pieces. So we're trying to have a true understanding of the order of events and what happened. And we probably need to go over a few more things for you to try to explain it the best you can. With the 35 years in between and stuff like that. So, the bar. That's where you meet her.

She wants to leave. She wants to go to your house, where you're staying on Elmcrest. You all have sex. Then afterward Bobby and Ralph come over for a little. They leave. She wants to leave. You're having an argument about it. Were you trying to get her to have sex again?

Wells: Yes. They were trying to take her home. She didn't want to go with them.

Harnett: Did she know them?

Wells: No. We just met. It's a coincidence we went to school together.

Mallett: So they offered her a ride. She didn't want to go with them.

Wells: She stayed a little longer.

Mallett: You wanted to have sex again?

Wells: Yes.

Harnett: She had all her clothes on? Everything on?

Mallett: Then the argument happens?

Wells: Then it was forceful. Then I realized what I'd done.

Mallett: I think we kind of heard two different things.

Harnett: If what we're understanding is wrong, correct us.

Mallett: We want this to be the truth about what happened.

Wells: Then I struck her. With the cutting board.

Harnett: Did you have sex with her after you struck her?

Wells: After strangulation. I knew that she was hurt and I just ... I knew it was bad ... so I strangled her.

Harnett: In front of her? Behind her?

Wells: I think I was on top of her.

Harnett: Were you clothed?

Wells: Partially clothed. I don't know. It's something I've tried not to remember.

Mallett: So she slaps you, you hit her in the head, she goes down and at that point, you ... start to have sex? Then you realize during that?

Wells: I realized it was serious, yeah.

Mallett: Did you hit her, strangle her, then have sex with her? Basically, after she was dead.

Wells: That was the thought. I hit her in the head and then choked her.

Harnett: So you tried to have sex with her again after that? Did you try and insert your penis in her again after that?

Wells: Yeah, I think I did.

Harnett: So your pants were down? Were they down when you hit her initially? So you struck her, strangled her and tried to have sex with her? Did you succeed at all?

Wells: No.

Harnett: So the argument was about she wanted to go home and you wanted to have sex with her.

Mallett: So here's ... we want to be honest with you. We know stuff. Evidence tells us things. There's one thing about this version that's not quite fitting the evidence. We talked about that towel. That towel came from the house. Because of the dogs and animals, there's black dog hair on the towel. But it's also in her mouth. Which leads me to believe that the towel or something was pushed in her mouth at some point. That goes back to hitting her in the head, starting to have sex with her then using a towel to make her quiet, then having sex with her, then strangling her.

Wells: Well, maybe that.

Mallett: Look, Dan, again, I don't want to put words in your mouth. Explain it to me.

Wells: I just don't know about the towel.

Harnett: The other thing is ... the pantyhose. You take them off. That towel, there's also your semen on there if you wiped yourself off. That makes sense the first time. Or the second time. Or you could've used the same towel to clean up the first time.

Mallett: Is that something you usually do after sex?

Wells: Use a towel to clean up, yeah. Or take a shower.

Harnett: Nothing will shock us. Did you masturbate after she was dead?

Wells: No.

Harnett: Do you remember the towel?

Mallett: There had to be a mess. A head wound bleeds. Did you have a hard time cleaning it up? Did your roommate come back and ask, "What is this?"

Harnett: How did you resolve the mess?

Wells: Just wiped up what I saw.

Harnett: Was she standing away from you or toward you?

Wells: She turned around. She hit me and I snapped. I realized I hit her so hard —

Mallett: She went straight down?

Wells: Yes.

Harnett: What was the catalyst? Why did you hit her?

Wells: Little argument or something ... words or whatever ... then she just reacted.

Harnett: Did you grab her first?

Wells: I might have grabbed her by her arm. She hit me. I lost it.

Mallett: Ever since then ... now, you kind of opened up this area of this personality that you didn't even know you had. I think everybody has that in them ... just what button got pushed that brings it out, that night you found that button. Ever go to that place again?

Wells: No. Just that one time.

Mallett: So this was about the anger or the sex?

Wells: I was angry because I got hit. Just reacted. Didn't know what else to do.

Mallett: Hit her, strangle her, try to have sex with her again. You actually do know —

Wells: I think it was being high on cocaine.

Mallett: You don't know that she's dead until in the process of having sex with her ... you realize she could be dead. Did you check her again?

Wells: Yes.

Mallett: To your knowledge, at that time, is that when she died?

Harnett: One thing doesn't match up ... need you to clarify. Some of her injuries occurred after she died. Whether that be from where you moved her or left her. They occurred before she died. The head injury. The neck injury. Both before she died. The way someone bleeds after they die ... you can tell the difference. She also had injuries before her death. She has injuries on her legs and on her pantyhose ... nail marks down her pantyhose. Those happened before she died. That means someone pulled them down before she was strangled. Those are different from the ones after she died. Because she has those as well. That seems you tried to have sex with her against her will before you strangled her.

Wells: That sounds right. I hit her. I wanted to have sex with her again. So I was trying to get her clothes off.

Mallett: She was still fighting?

Wells: Maybe. Not a lot.

Harnett: I can tell you the head injury wasn't enough to kill her. When someone goes completely unconscious, there's a major brain injury. Knock someone out they probably have a concussion. We see external trauma but it doesn't transfer to her brain. So it means she's still conscious in some aspect. And I know because of the injuries on her legs and [tears] to the pantyhose that she was struggling.

Mallett: If you're just pulling them off, she won't have those injuries. But I want to be very careful. I don't want to put words in your mouth.

Wells: If that's what you have, that's what happened.

Harnett: Well, we want you to explain it. We don't want to put words in your mouth. Absolutely don't want to do that.

Mallett: Hit in the head. Dazed. You take her pantyhose off.

Wells: She's still struggling a little bit ... had sex with her ... then finished it.

Mallett: I'm still struggling with that. You're right, strangulation was how she died. The injuries don't match what you're saying.

Wells: I could've had a belt or something. I don't remember. I strangled her.

Mallett: So you were on top of her?

Wells: On top of her and she's on her side.

Mallett: You got in this position because you wanted to have sex with her. She's struggling. Making you angry. The injuries don't match that you strangled her with your hands.

Wells: Could have been a belt or something.

Harnett: Are you sure when you're fighting you didn't put anything in her mouth?

Wells: I don't recall. I don't remember. I guess if there's dog hair in her mouth, then I did it.

Mallett: Well, we don't know. These are just scenarios. It could have been from the floor. If she was face down on the floor.

Wells: Could've been that.

Mallett: One other thing. When you say you left her on the side of the road, you make it sound almost gentle.

Wells: It wasn't gentle. I just dragged her out of the truck.

Mallett: There were injuries on her arm like she got drug. There's a big scrape on her arm.

Wells: I was out all the way over the curb.

Mallett: When you took her out of the house?

Wells: I carried her.

Mallett: Didn't drop her? There were strange injuries. Large bruise on the forearm. Big scrape.

Wells: Might have been. Dragged her or squeezed her. I can't remember what caused her arm all that damage.

Mallett: One other thing that complicates this a little bit. Remember when [Harnett] said the thing about the phone call? There was another girl killed three months later.

Harnett: To the day.

Mallett: Her body was left similarly ... on the road, on the west side of
Pensacola. Not far from where you live now.

Wells: No. Don't know anything about that. On Cerny Road?

Mallett: Well, you didn't live there at the time. It's a coincidence you
live there now. There was a phone call trying to take credit for the
incidents. Wouldn't be doing our job if we didn't ask. Similar done.
They looked similar. Similar lifestyle.

Harnett: Similar manner.

(*Mallett puts a picture of Patricia Stephens in front of Wells. Stephens
was found raped and murdered — strangled to death in Pensacola
on March 1, 1985.*)

Wells: I don't know her.

Harnett: So with her, there's also DNA recovered. This other investigator who has this case has your name and we're waiting to compare
the DNA to see if it comes back to a match. We accept that people
get themselves into these situations. Your ability to explain that one
if it comes back as a match undoes a lot of the good you did today ...
it throws out some of our stories about you not being that monster. If
you are involved in anything else ... you're known now.

Mallett: Part of our job is going to Missouri now. Wherever you've
lived. And you're going into the national database now. If there's going to be something else that pops up, the best thing is to get ahead
of the game now. Start narrowing that focus and save people some
time. Any other place you lived or passed through where something
like this might have happened?

Wells: There's not. It's just that one night. I know it's not good.

Harnett: We don't want someone to classify you as something you're
not if there's another case. This is the opportunity to explain it now
... they'll know you've already had the chance to explain it here. Your
ability to understand and explain it like that is gone.

Mallett: What happened tonight is we had to convince you through
the evidence that you had to tell the truth. You don't want to do that
again. That takes away from some of your sincerity. It looks like you
weren't trying to get it off your chest after 35 years. You're convinced
you're done and you try to save yourself. It's not about you being
remorseful ... it's about you saving yourself. This image we have now
goes away ... if there's another case it's no longer that. You don't seem
remorseful. It'll be bad. The Patricia Stephens case. It's similar. Same
time frame. There's DNA there.

Wells: It's not mine. I'm being totally honest with you. This was a one-time major faux pas. I've had remorse forever ... it's just ... it's horrible.

Mallett: I'll let you know I already called her son. He broke down in a big way. Missed out on a lot.

Wells: He missed out on a lot. He missed out on everything.

Mallett: Because you had an angry moment. It's good you're taking responsibility now, but you worry me. I worry about the other cases.

18

OLD DOGS

Mallett and Harnett spent approximately three hours talking with Wells. When they were done, they asked him what he wanted to do with his truck. Wells said his older sister, Nan, who lived a few houses down from him, could pick it up from the police impound yard. Wells asked if he could make a few phone calls. Mallett gave him his cell-phone back and left him alone.

First, Wells called his employer, CDC Woodworking, and spoke with a co-worker, Warren Weidamoyer, to tell him he wouldn't be coming back to work. Wells told Weidamoyer he'd been arrested for committing a murder "from a long time ago" and asked him to make sure his extensive collection of valuable woodworking equipment went to his son. The next call was to his older sister, Nan.

✿ ✿ ✿

Nan Wells: Hey, Honey.

Daniel Wells: Hey Nan. I need you to listen to me about this I did something 35 years ago ... I committed homicide. I'm getting ready to go to county and get booked there. It's two detectives. They got

my DNA and they've been following me for a while. A couple of
months I guess.

Nan Wells: Don't talk to anybody.

Daniel Wells: I've already told them. They've known. I'm accepting
responsibility for it. I should've come clean a long time ago. I'm sorry.
Do you have —

Nan Wells: Don't apologize. Just hold on. Hold on.

Daniel Wells: I need you to get Morgan.

Nan Wells: You can get bailed out, Dan. You can get bailed out, sweet-
heart. We'll talk about it.

Daniel Wells: The warrant has no bond on it. Tomorrow I'm going to
make my first appearance. There won't be a bond. I've been living
with it for 35 years ... and it's not good. I love you.

Nan Wells: Oh, Dan. I love you, Dan.

Daniel Wells: I need you to get in touch with Morgan for me. I'll probably never see him again.

Nan Wells: I will. This is not the end. This is just the beginning of a
procedure. Dan listen to me ... do you want me to call Carol?

Daniel Wells: Better than finding out on the news. I don't have my
will, but I've left everything to Morgan. I know he knows that.

Nan Wells: I'm dying —

Daniel Wells: I'm going to spend the rest of my life in prison. I would
rather not have life ... you gotta take care of all this for me.

Nan Wells: I will, Dan.

Daniel Wells: Thank you. I don't deserve that.

❊ ❊ ❊

Heintzelman took fingerprints and a cheek swab from Wells in the
interview room. It was a job normally reserved for assistant analysts.

"We had just put so much time and energy into trying to get justice
for this woman that I wanted to be the one to do it," Heintzelman
said. "[Wells] was much more meek than I had envisioned he would
be. He kind of felt like a broken man at that point. I expected him to
be this monster and he was very compliant, very polite. Not what I
envisioned. You kind of expect horns to be coming out of his head, but
he wasn't just an outright monster like I thought he'd be. I gave him
instructions and he said 'Yes ma'am' and that was it."

The final person to talk with Wells that day was Escambia County Sheriff's Office cold case investigator James Lee, who had the unsolved Patricia Stephens murder from March 1985 as part of his caseload. Lee's questioning went nowhere, which made sense because anyone who looked at Wells could tell the 57-year-old was in shock.

After Lee finished, Mallett and Harnett handcuffed Wells and walked him back out the way he came in and into a waiting Pensacola Police Department SUV to take him to the Escambia County Jail. As Wells was driven away, Mallett kissed his wife and hugged his daughter. Heintzelman and Connors hugged and cried. Harnett stood to the side and took it all in.

"Fucking incredible," he said, shaking his head. "Just fucking incredible."

After a few minutes, the group looked around at each other, smiles stuck on their faces and tears streaming down some of their cheeks. No one spoke, and they all found their attention slowly drawn to the clear, night sky, where stars seemed to fill up every inch of space.

※ ※ ※

Back inside the station, Mallett went into his office and logged Wells' arrest into the police department's official database. This would make the arrest and his task force's work part of the public record for the first time. Once Mallett logged into the system, the list of his most recent arrests popped up on the screen. The last arrest in the database credited to Mallett was from 2014 — six years prior — which was the same year he moved to a full-time administrative role.

"Been a minute," Mallett remarked. "Probably be the last one before I retire."

Later that night, a small group met in the Major Cases Room, where someone broke out a bottle of bourbon. It was a tradition reserved for closing only the biggest cases. When it was time for the man who replaced Mallett as the head of the investigations unit, Kevin Christman, to give a toast, he raised his glass toward Mallett and Harnett.

"Here's to old dogs," Christman said. "I guess you can teach them new tricks."

Tonya Ethridge McKinley at 23 years old, 1984.
Source: Public records request.

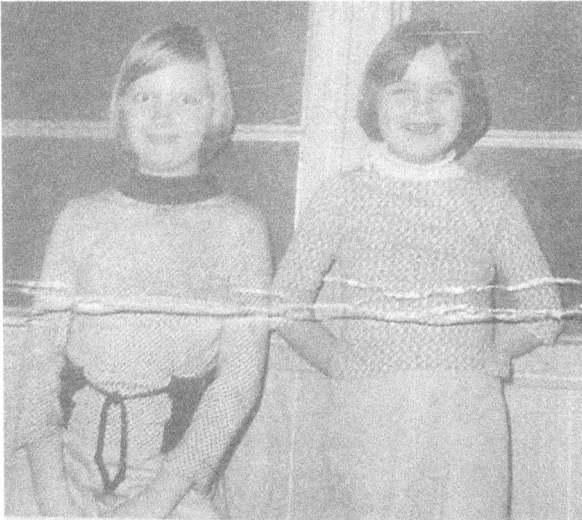

Tonya Ethridge McKinley and Renee Ethridge, 1965.
Photo courtesy of Renee McCall.

Patricia Stephens.
Photo courtesy of Florida Department of Law Enforcement.

Chuck Mallett, 1996.
Photo courtesy of Chuck Mallett.

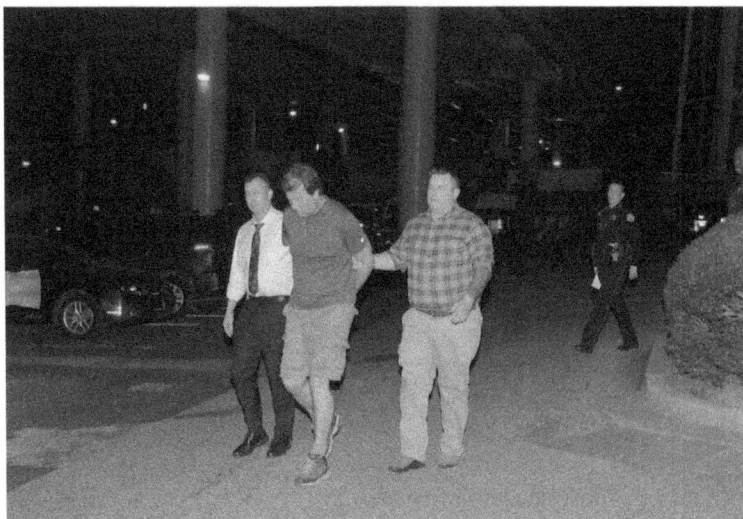

Chuck Mallett and Danny Harnett walking Daniel Wells out in handcuffs, March 18, 2020.
Photo courtesy of Heather Mallett.

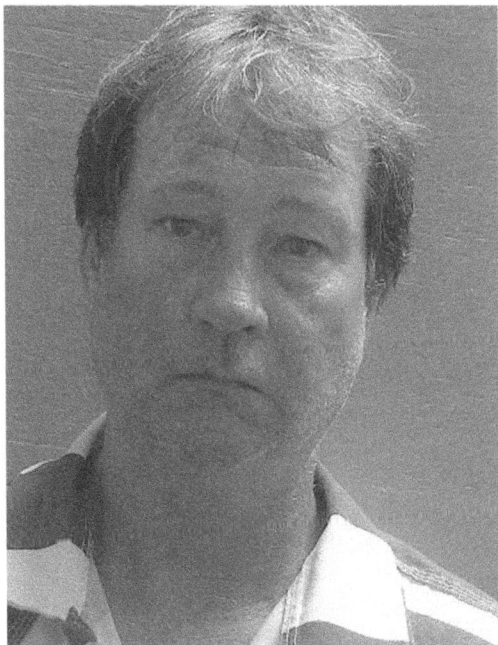

Daniel Wells' mug shot.
Pensacola Police Department.

Chuck Mallett and Danny Harnett.
Photo courtesy of the author.

19

THE PHARMACIST'S SON

The morning after the arrest, Mallett took a small group of Tonya's family and friends into the Major Cases Room to give them a few details on how they caught Wells before the police held a press conference to formally announce the arrest. Afterward, Mallett said, there would be a small, private reception in memory of Tonya that was for her family and the people who worked on the case. Tim Jr. drove overnight from Georgia to be there. Renee and her youngest son were also there, as were Carolynn Stephens and James Enterkin.

Police Chief Tommi Lyter spoke first at the press conference, calling the case "justice delayed, not justice denied," and gave a brief overview of the investigation. He thanked the Florida Department of Law Enforcement for its help and spotlighted Mallett for solving the oldest cold case in Northwest Florida history. Pensacola Mayor Grover Robinson also spoke, as did Florida State Attorney Bill Eddins, who announced the state was proceeding with first-degree murder and first-degree rape charges while Wells was being held without bond in the Escambia County Jail. This was perhaps the first signal the state was going to pursue the death penalty for Wells, who had his first court appearance scheduled for April 8, 2020.

One person who didn't make it to Pensacola was Vanita, who now lived in Texas. As news began to filter out that morning about the arrest, she began sending text messages to friends, family and acquaintances, including Renee, to say the picture of Tonya being used by the police and in the news reports wasn't her. In the picture, Tonya is looking directly into the camera and is shown from the shoulders up and dressed for a night out. She looks stunning.

Vanita made no mention of Wells, the arrest or the case finally being solved after 35 years. Just the picture.

❖ ❖ ❖

In the week following Wells' arrest, four women came forward with what seemed like different versions of the same story about their interactions with him. All asked to remain anonymous.

"He was creepy," said a former co-worker. "Something was off about him. When he looked at you, it just gave you the chills. He looked at you like you weren't a human. You didn't want him to put any of his focus on you at any time, ever. He was known as a real woman hater. He raged about an ex who'd ruined his life. And I mean he *really* raged. She was the cause of everything wrong in his life."

Another woman who knew Wells through one of her exes called him out in front of a group of people for how badly he talked about women. Wells turned on her. It got ugly.

"He hated strong women," she said. "If you stood up to him and told him he was making you feel uncomfortable, he would belittle you and bad-mouth you to anyone who would listen. After time I became very afraid of him."

Mallett kept pulling on threads in anticipation of having to testify at a trial. One of those brought him back to the house on Elmcrest Drive where Wells raped and murdered Tonya.

During his interview with police, Wells said the house belonged to a man named John Pendergrast when he lived there. Property records showed the man's name wasn't John Pendergrast, but John Kirtz, and when Mallett ran Kirtz's name through the system he was shocked to find out he died on January 2, 1985 — one day after Tonya was murdered. Wells made no mention of his roommate's death during his interview, so this brought a scenario into play where Wells may have killed Tonya and then killed Kirtz to cover up the crime. Several days later, Mallett spoke with Kirtz's sister; she said her brother was sick for quite some time leading up to his death and, as far as the family knew, he died in his sleep.

Mallett was waiting for Wells' older sister, Nan, when she came to the police station to pick up her brother's truck, but she refused to speak with him. Mallett reached out to both of Wells' ex-wives but didn't hear back. In the week following his arrest, several of Wells' neighbors reached out to Renee via Facebook Messenger to tell her there was a "fire sale" of Wells' woodworking equipment and personal items going on at his house.

Even with all of his work, the one thing Mallett and his team agreed on was that the most insight anyone on his team was getting into Wells came from the jailhouse conversations he was having with Nan, via phone and in person, and all were being recorded.

✵ ✵ ✵

There wasn't much, if anything, remarkable or memorable about Daniel Wells growing up. He graduated from Milton High School in 1981, and his classmates seemed to remember him almost solely because of his height and because his father, Rodney Wells, owned a pharmacy in Milton called The Prescription Shop. Wells' mother left him and his four sisters when he was 13 years old to be with a man in Atmore, Alabama. Both of his parents eventually remarried and his mother died in the late 1990s. His father died in 2002.

In March 1990, Wells was working as a shift manager at Trout Auto Parts in Pensacola when one of its employees, Robin Archer, was fired for stealing. Archer blamed Wells for ratting him out and vowed to get revenge, no matter how long it took. In January 1991, Archer finally got his opportunity when his teenage cousin, Patrick Bonifay, came over with two of his friends, Eddie Barth and Larry Fordham, looking to borrow money. Archer said he would pay the three of them $250 — total, not each — to kill Wells. They agreed to do it, and Archer instructed them to go to Trout Auto Parts while Wells was working that night.

"Make it look like a robbery," Archer said, "not a hit."

That night, the three teenagers went to the store and stood outside with a gun but lost their nerve. The next day they went back to Archer and asked for the cash again. They were told if they wanted the money they needed to kill Wells and make it look like a robbery. That night, the trio returned to the auto parts store right before closing time, went up to the man at the front register and asked him for something on the wall behind the counter. When the man turned back around, Bonifay shot him twice in the abdomen. Fordham and Bonifay jumped over the counter to rob the cash register and as they were struggling with the register's locking system, Bonifay noticed the man was still alive and trying to crawl away.

The man pleaded for his life, telling the teenagers he had a wife and small children at home.

"Enough about your fucking wife and kids," Bonifay said right before he walked over and shot 36-year-old Billy Wayne Coker twice in his left temple.

They had killed the wrong man.

Just hours before the start of his shift that night, Wells asked Coker to cover for him because he was sick. Coker, who lived with his wife and three kids in a mobile home less than a mile from the store, always jumped at the opportunity to pick up more hours. Just one year earlier, Coker and his family were homeless and living out of his car, so his part-time job at the auto parts store was a lifeline. Wells was the one who trained Coker to work at the store and was close enough with the family that Coker's kids called him "Uncle Dan" sometimes.

Within days, all four of the people involved with Coker's murder were under arrest. Barth and Fordham were convicted and received life sentences. Archer received a death sentence and so did Bonifay, who at 17 years old became the youngest death penalty convict in Florida history. In 2017, the U.S. Supreme Court overturned Bonifay's death penalty conviction because he was under 18 years old at the time of the murder, and it converted his sentence to life without the possibility of parole. Barth, who had also been under 18 years old, saw his sentence reduced to 26 years and was released with time served.

Over the years, Wells consistently bragged to friends and co-workers about his involvement in the case, pointing out how he'd barely escaped death. In the week before his first scheduled court appearance, both Connors and Mallett voiced concerns Wells was a suicide risk.

"He's not saying he's going to do it, it's just the way he's been talking," Mallett said. "I don't think things are going really well for him in jail."

❀ ❀ ❀

The emergency 911 call went out from the Escambia County Jail shortly before 5 a.m. on April 2, 2020, with a report of an unresponsive inmate in his cell. Sometime during the night, Wells committed suicide. Mallett found out early enough that he was able to call both Renee and Tim Jr. to let them know before the story hit the news, and both of them were devastated at losing the chance to finally confront Tonya's killer face-to-face. The suicide also closed the door on any chance Tonya's family had to file a wrongful death lawsuit against Wells, which was an avenue Tim Jr. and Renee were both already exploring. Wells' most valuable asset was his home in Pensacola, which he purchased for $60,000 in 2011 and his son, Morgan, sold for $120,000 in March 2021.

In jail conversations with his older sister, Wells talked several times about how he and his siblings endured serious physical abuse from their mother beginning when they were around 7 or 8 years old, and mostly when she was drunk. Wells said he'd been sexually abused as a child by someone outside of the family and intimated his sisters had been abused in a similar manner. Wells told his sister he sometimes "snapped" as a result of his childhood trauma.

The idea Wells may have killed again continued to haunt the task force.

"I agree with the idea that it does seem like if someone does something like [murder] and gets away with it, that behavior can repeat itself," Connors said. "And we found the stuff he'd done, mostly. In Missouri, the interesting thing was we knew after he killed Tonya he'd had run-ins with the law, but they'd purged records over time.

We knew he'd only been charged twice for exposing himself, but in 1998 he had two different counts of doing that and one of sexual battery, and there were two different victims. It seemed like after that there's literally nothing else. He just stopped exposing himself. That was around the same time he had his son."

In the weeks following his arrest, one thing Wells remained adamant about was getting his affairs in order. He granted Nan power of attorney, had her find the deed to his home, and set up a trust in his son's name. Despite his sister's pleading, he insisted no money be spent on his legal defense. Nan believed the right attorney could lead to a reduced sentence.

"He just said, 'No I belong here, [Tonya] had a kid,'" Connors said. "I also think he didn't want his sister to waste money because he knew what he was going to do. He would call and thank his sister for everything she'd done and tell her he appreciated her. At first, on his calls, he sounded really calm ... like 'OK, I did this and this is what I've done to myself,' but as time went on it really started to sink in. You're never leaving jail. You're going to be here forever because you've ruined so many lives. You're never going to get out."

Wells only talked to three people during his short time in jail: his sister, his son and a friend from work. Out of his four sisters, Wells only spoke with Nan after his arrest and tried to get in touch with Morgan's mother, who was his first ex-wife, but she never responded.

After Wells' suicide, Harnett was asked to debrief the Escambia County Sheriff's Office on Tonya's murder and the investigation that led to an arrest. Part of the debrief included trading information on the murder of Patricia Stephens. When he was directly asked if he thought Wells may have been responsible for both murders, Harnett was skeptical.

"I know there's another case that happened a few months after this, and it's a leap, but it's possible," Harnett said. "It's also possible [Wells] got really skilled at doing this, realized his shortcomings, continued to be a murderer and maybe did it a few more times. There's still DNA in the [Stephens] case that hasn't been compared yet."

Part of Harnett's process was trying to build a picture of what happened the night of Tonya's murder based on the physical evidence and the confession from Wells. For all of the work done on the case, it's probably as close as anyone will ever come to understanding what actually happened that night.

"[Wells] said they had consensual sex, but I don't believe that and no one within the investigation believes that," Harnett said. "What did make sense was that he met her at Darryl's, agreed to take her home and took her to his house instead and things went sideways. When he says they had consensual sex, then he hit her in the back of the head, strangled her and killed her ... that doesn't make sense at all. She has fresh, antemortem injuries on her leg where her panty-hose was pulled down and she was bleeding. Well, that wouldn't have happened to her in consensual sex. And it wouldn't have happened after she was strangled and murdered. That means he was trying to rape her before she was dead, so that would be after he hit her in the head but before the strangulation. He can't strangle her and cause those types of injuries to her leg at the same time."

20

THE RETIREMENT PARTY

The recording of the phone call Mallett placed to Tim Jr. following the arrest was posted on the police department's Facebook page the next day and quickly went viral. It was shared over 1,000 times in the next 24 hours as Mallett found himself inundated with calls and messages of congratulations from former colleagues as well as people he'd never met. As always, he was able to bring some much-needed perspective to what was happening around him.

"You don't get too many opportunities to solve a case from 35 years ago," Mallett said. "But to me, at the end of the day, someone still lost their life. Someone still lost their mother. They don't ever get past that, so you don't ever get past that."

At the beginning of the investigation, Mallett said he planned to retire within the next four or five years, which meant either 2023 or 2024. For almost his whole career he'd worked under the belief that being a cop meant you walked away with a case hanging over your head. Carolynn Stephens once said every cop had a "white whale" they took with them. No one ever got away clean.

Somehow, Mallett seemed like he just might.

"I still love my job, I still love coming to work every day," Mallett said in the summer of 2020. "But the work we do, once I retire, I have no interest in continuing it afterward. A lot of guys that retire stay involved in police work part-time, or they work extra-duty jobs that become full-time jobs, but I'm not interested in doing that. When I'm ready to walk away, that will be it."

Fifteen months after solving Tonya's case, Mallett announced he was going to retire from the police force and take a job as the director of security for Ascension Sacred Heart, a company which owned and operated four large hospitals along Florida's Gulf Coast.

✧ ✧ ✧

On August 1, 2021, Mallett's retirement party was held at a tiny dive bar on Pensacola Beach called The Islander, which claimed to be the "oldest bar on the beach," and where sunburned, boozy tourists and locals had been served and overserved since 1958.

Mallett's friends and family rented out the upstairs portion of the bar, which opened up to a large balcony where you could see waves rolling in off the Gulf of Mexico. Mallett and Harnett held court at the bar for hours, tossing stories back and forth about cases they'd worked and cops they'd worked with. That included several stories about Adam McCoy, who'd been one of the first detectives Mallett consulted with on Tonya's case. McCoy retired just weeks before Wells' arrest and committed suicide one month later. McCoy, who was 53 years old, fought a private battle with severe anxiety and PTSD that dated back decades, to his time serving in the Gulf War in 1991 through his 26 years as a cop.

One of Mallett's initiatives after he went into administration was a greater focus on mental health for officers, who he felt too often internalized work trauma or dealt with their problems with drugs or alcohol until it spilled over into their personal and professional lives. McCoy's suicide was another reminder that for all the work that had been done concerning cops and mental health, there was still more to do.

✧ ✧ ✧

In September 2021, Mallett went to a rented loft in downtown Pensacola and spent the day filming interviews for an episode of the true-crime television series "Cold Case Files" about Tonya's murder. The popular show was rebooted by the A&E Network and Netflix after being off the air full-time since 2006 and following a surge in viewership of old episodes during the pandemic.

For the episode, which aired in February 2022, producers also filmed interviews with Renee, Tim Jr., Vanita, Heintzelman, Tonya's mother, Laverne and investigative journalist Tony Adame, who'd secretly been given complete and total access to the investigation by Mallett from its first days in 2019 through the arrest of Wells in March 2020 in a unique, information-sharing agreement between the two that was only known to those in the investigation's inner circle.

Throughout the afternoon of his interview, Mallett recounted his experience investigating Tonya's murder from start to finish, going over the entire history of the case, including every twist and turn that led him and his team to Wells' doorstep as he solved the oldest cold case in Northwest Florida history.

"I can't explain the forces that brought us all together," Mallett said. "I look back at that time and there was nothing else to indicate that it was time for this case to be reinvestigated. So it was just happenstance ... and maybe a little bit of God's hand that brought us all together."

EPILOGUE

In the fall of 2018, I was the sports editor at the *Pensacola News Journal*, and part of my job required me to be the weekend editor for the entire newspaper and its website once a month. This meant I was responsible for the Sunday and Monday editions making it to press on time and for updating the paper's website. As the sports editor, I already worked most weekends, so the weekend editor shifts didn't require much extra work on my part aside from keeping an eye out for breaking news and being available in case a news reporter needed my help. Nine months of the year I was going to be there anyway.

One weekend, the newspaper's executive editor, who was my boss, told me if there was no breaking news that came up over the weekend, she wanted me to ask the two news reporters working if they wanted to team up on an "evergreen" feature the paper could use in the future at any given date. I had a vague idea for a story on cold cases in the area, but when I went to talk with the reporters that weekend, they made it clear they weren't interested. One of the paper's veteran reporters who was also working that weekend — Kevin Robinson — got to witness the rejection firsthand and approached me after I got back to my desk.

"There's a website," he said, gesturing to my laptop. "I'll show you."

Robinson directed me to the Florida Department of Law Enforcement website, which had a special section with a slideshow of 70 cold cases from every part of Florida, with pictures of the victims and a summary of the circumstances of the case underneath each one. Robinson believed the site would have a few cases from our area among them. He was right.

I took notes on the half-dozen cases with ties to Northwest Florida and began to research them through the newspaper archives. One of the local cases that caught my attention was the murder of 29-year-old Patricia Stephens on March 1, 1985. She had been raped, strangled to death and dumped half-naked on the side of the road in Pensacola. Going further back in the archives, I found something not mentioned on the FDLE website. Patricia was the second woman murdered in Pensacola in two months, following Tonya Ethridge McKinley on January 1, 1985. Both women had been killed in almost the same fashion and both were pretty brunettes with long hair who were in their 20s. Most crucially, 33 years later, both cases remained unsolved.

Because Tonya was killed first, and since I was working off the initial premise the two murders might be connected, it seemed prudent to focus my efforts on her case to begin with. I put together a short presentation for the next editorial staff meeting, and when I got the chance to pitch my story, it was met with silence. Halfway through, the executive editor turned to look at the news editor, who rejected my idea out of hand.

"It's not even really a story," she said.

A few days later, I taped together three large maps of Escambia County, Santa Rosa County and Okaloosa County — the entire Pensacola metropolitan area plus one more county to the east — and pinned them to the wall in my dining room to get a larger perspective. I used Post-it Notes — blue for solved and orange for unsolved — to mark all the spots in the three counties where dead girls had been found over the last 50 years in manners even remotely similar to Tonya's and wrote the names of the victims and dates of the crimes on the Post-its. I wrote a rough outline of what I thought the project might look like as a book or a podcast and told myself not to worry about finding a home for it — just to get to work on it and see what happened.

Through a combination of newspaper archives, online public records and social media, I put together a preliminary list of Tonya's family and friends I wanted to interview. Right before Christmas 2018, I began to reach out to some of the people on the list. The most receptive of those was Tonya's older sister, Renee, who created a Facebook page in 2012 called the "Tonya Ethridge McKinley Memorial Page" that she'd kept active since, never letting more than a month or so go by without a new post. Sometimes she pleaded for information on her sister's murder. Sometimes she just used the page to talk about how much she missed Tonya.

I met with Renee for the first time at her mobile home in Jay, Florida, on January 3, 2019, just two days after the 35th anniversary of her sister's murder. We sat in her kitchen and talked about her life, Tonya's life and the multiple investigations that had taken place over the years. Renee had family pictures and an extensive record of her correspondence with law enforcement, media, family and friends about Tonya's case dating back decades, and she shared all of it with me. When I left, the last thing Renee told me was that she knew she'd probably die before she found out who killed her sister, but she couldn't live with herself if she stopped trying to find out who did it.

I thought it was one of the most amazing, admirable, heartbreaking things I'd ever heard.

❊ ❊ ❊

A few weeks later, I woke up to an early-morning phone call from my boss and someone from human resources telling me I was being laid off as part of company-wide cuts. After I filled out some paperwork online, I received a severance package equal to approximately three months' salary. With quite a bit of time on my hands, I decided right away I wanted to use as much of it as I could to work on my story about the murders of Tonya and Patricia.

❊ ❊ ❊

In April 2019, after I felt I'd squeezed every piece of information out of the sources I found on my own, I made my first contact with the Pensacola police. Kristin Brown was still listed as the head of the Criminal Investigations Division on the department's website, but when I called her she informed me Chuck Mallett took over for her as the head of CID in January. She told me former PPD Captain Paul Kelly, who now worked for the FDLE, was the last one to work on Tonya's case, which I already knew because of Renee's emails. Brown gave me a cellphone number for Kelly, but he made it clear when we spoke that he wouldn't talk with me about Tonya's case, even on background. My next step was to file a Freedom of Information Act (FOIA) request with the Pensacola Police for access to the entirety of Tonya's case file.

Within a few days of sending the request, I received a return email from the police informing me I was being denied access to the files because it was still an ongoing, active investigation. This meant the police did not have to comply with open-records requests other than to send me the initial, two-page report filed by Officer Ken Franks the morning Tonya's body was found. According to Florida's open-records laws, criminal investigations could only still be deemed active if they were still "reasonably working toward an arrest or a conviction," which didn't feel like it could reasonably be applied to a 35-year-old investigation that had, to that point, resulted in zero arrests.

I sent an email response that stated my concerns as plainly and politely as possible, and at the end I added a personal plea. I explained how Tonya's family believed there might be DNA from her killer taken from under her fingernails, but they'd never actually been told this. Their belief was mostly based on the state of her body when she was found and that they all assumed she'd fought for her life. In the case there was DNA, I asked the police to please consider using the same genetic genealogy method of detection used to capture the Golden State Killer in California in April 2018. One week later, on April 22, 2019, I received a short email response from a police administrative assistant with Mallett's cellphone number and was instructed to call him if I had further questions about the case. I left Mallett a voicemail later that day.

I spent the next few weeks picking apart the initial offense report and continued to speak with Tonya's friends and family. While the report was just a small part of what I'd initially sought access to, it still included a wealth of new information like the names and addresses of the three people who found Tonya's body and what I assumed was their old address on Peacock Drive. A quick Google search indicated Franks had been retired for some time but still lived in Pensacola and not far from where Tonya's body was found. I called the listed home phone number for him and received a call back from a private number within minutes. It was Franks.

"What the hell are you calling me for?" he asked. "What's this all about?"

Once I was able to explain who I was and some of the specifics about Tonya's murder, he softened a little bit. He said he remembered the case well and agreed to meet me the next day at his home, where he said we could talk in his driveway so we didn't disturb his wife.

Franks and I met in person the next day — in his driveway — and while he seemed mostly annoyed at my presence, he was still willing to answer a few questions. He remembered two things very clearly about that morning. The first was that it was obvious to him Tonya was dead from the moment he saw her body. The second was that his first call that morning had been to Crime Scene Supervisor Bob Grant.

"[Grant] was always my first call," Franks said.

After speaking with Franks, I went to Peacock Drive, to the spot where Tonya's body had been found. Public records told me that the house listed on the police report at 4830 Peacock Drive no longer belonged to Mary Lloyd, and Dr. James Lloyd had died in 2000. I still knocked on the front door with the hope whoever lived there might know what happened to the Lloyds. As I was standing at the door, the woman who owned the home pulled her car into the driveway and got out to speak with me. I told her I was a journalist looking into a murder from the mid-1980s where the woman's body was dumped in the empty lot just a few feet from where we were standing.

"Oh, I know all about that," she said. "Mary told us about it when we bought the house from her. It's actually still pretty well known in the neighborhood. About what happened to the girl, I mean."

"Do you mean Mary Lloyd?" I asked.

"That's her," she said. "We bought the house from her a few years ago. She also owned the lot next door and built a house there. That's where she lives now but she's pretty old so if you go up and knock on the door and she doesn't answer just leave a note or something. She doesn't ever really answer the door unless her son is with her."

I thanked her and followed the instructions, leaving a note explaining who I was and what I was trying to get information about and including my cellphone number. The next day I received a call from Mary's son, who asked me if I was going to pay him for an interview with his mother, which I was not. Mary, who was in her 80s, called me the next day and apologized for her son's call and said she didn't know he was going to ask me for money. She said she had trouble getting around because of her age, but her memory was still razor sharp and she remembered every detail from the morning she found Tonya's body. We ended up talking for two hours, and it was obvious she was still deeply bothered by what she'd seen that night.

Mary agreed to speak with me again if I needed her and gave me contact information for her daughter, Sherry, but said she didn't think she'd speak with me because she suffered from "severe memory loss issues." She was right. I sent several messages to Sherry's former boyfriend, Jeffrey Pierce, but he never responded.

On May 18, 2019 — my birthday — I met with Vanita's ex-husband, Larry Winchester, at a coffee shop in Pensacola. Almost right off the bat, he asked me who I thought killed Tonya. I said her family mostly thought it was Tim Davidson and it seemed like there was a lot of circumstantial evidence to back that up. Even Tim's son, Tim Jr., was open to the idea it may have been his father.

"If that's what you think, then you're fucked," Larry said. "No way he did it."

"How can you be so sure?" I asked.

"Because he was a pussy," Larry said. "He backed down the moment anyone fought back, and Tonya always fought back. He's not a killer. If that's what you really think after spending all this time on this, then maybe you don't know shit."

"That's a distinct possibility," I said. "But that's why I'm talking to you, Larry."

We both laughed. I talked with him for another hour or so about Tonya, her murder and his life before and after Vanita left him for Tim. Like Mary, he agreed to speak with me again if needed. On May 22, which was exactly one month after I called him, Mallett returned my call and asked me to meet him for lunch the next day.

"It's nothing bad," Mallett said. "I think you'll probably like what I have to say."

We met at a diner in Pensacola called Jerry's and sat in a booth, where we both ordered bacon cheeseburgers, fries and Cokes. Mallett was tall and had a close-cropped flattop. He was dressed sharply in a checkered dress shirt, dark slacks and dark shoes, with his badge and gun sitting on his hip. He asked me about writing about sports, which I'd almost exclusively done up to this point, and wanted to know why I was so interested in Tonya's murder.

A few months earlier, on a trip with friends to Daytona Beach, one of them asked me the same thing, and I didn't have a good answer. She told me I probably needed to have a better "why" moving forward because someone who mattered would eventually ask me.

She was right, and here it was.

"It doesn't seem fair," I told Mallett. "With her kid. It doesn't seem fair he didn't get to have a mom and she didn't get to raise her son."

We sat there in silence. Mallett leaned back and sized me up, not trying to hide what he was doing. After an uncomfortable few seconds, he made a gesture with his hands that seemed to indicate something between "Fuck it?" and "Why not?"

"I'm going to do something I've never done before," Mallett said, "something I don't think the Pensacola police have ever done before. I'm gonna let you in. I'm gonna give you what you want, I think."

Mallett told me he was reopening the investigation into Tonya's murder with a considerable amount of resources and manpower at his disposal, and from that point moving forward, if I wanted, I would have access to all of the police department's case files regarding Tonya as well as full access to a special task force he was putting together to try to solve Tonya's murder. The main thrust of the investigation would be using the genealogical testing method, which was the same one I suggested via email after my FOIA request was rejected, when, unbeknown to me, Mallett and Heintzelman had already put the wheels in motion.

"I don't want to get screwed," Mallett said. "You screw me over and we're done. This whole thing has to stay a secret or it won't work, but you filed that request at the exact right time."

Mallett made it clear I could not write anything about the case or tell anyone about my involvement until it was solved. Since there was no guarantee the case would ever be solved, I said I could commit to those parameters for one year, and at the end of that one year we would need to revisit things, which he agreed to. As a journalist, my urge was to not just agree to everything he wanted, but this type of access, to my knowledge, was almost unprecedented. It seemed like an unbelievable, once-in-a-lifetime break.

"Why are you doing this?" I asked.

"Sometimes we keep doing things the same way and it doesn't work," Mallett said. "In my mind, that means maybe we need to mix things up a bit ... and as a journalist, eventually there might be a question you can ask or a place you can go that we can't. So, you in?"

"Yeah," I said. "I'm in."

We shook hands on it and from that moment forward, I was embedded, for lack of a better term, with Mallett's investigation. Every meeting and every email. Every brainstorming session. Even on some days when there wasn't anything going on, I would stop by if Mallett or one of the other detectives wasn't busy just to see if there were little things I could pick up on.

The day Wells was arrested, I sat in Mallett's office and talked with him all morning. I ate lunch with him and sat shotgun in the unmarked car with him as we made small talk with Harnett in an empty parking lot, waiting for Wells to get off work. I watched Wells placed in the back of the police SUV through the front window of Mallett's SUV and made the ride back to the station, sirens wailing, where Maegan Mallett set up the link on the computer in her father's office so I could watch the interview with Wells.

That night, after everything was done, I sat with Mallett and Harnett in the Major Cases Room after everyone else was gone. The three of us drank bourbon and talked, deep into the night, letting the reality of what had happened begin to sink in. I'd grown especially fond of

Harnett, who had piercing blue eyes and reminded me of the cops from all the movies and TV shows I'd ever loved — barrel-chested, profane, funny and loyal.

"You ever do anything like this before?" Harnett asked me. "Chuck said you just mainly wrote about sports. Ever try to write about a murder before?"

"Nope," I said. "First time."

"What the fuck, man," Harnett said, laughing. "I mean, good for you, obviously, but also what in the actual fuck."

After the first meeting with Mallett, I started a journal to track my involvement in the investigation and updated it when anything even remotely significant happened with the case. I've included my personal journal here, as an appendix, but it's not compulsory reading. If you've come this far and you want extra context to the story, it's there for you. I've made minor changes to the journal to protect the names of confidential informants, anonymous sources or names found doing research into the genetic genealogy portion of the investigation, which was part of my agreement with Parabon and Mallett at the beginning of the investigation. I've also deleted some conversations that were off the record but were included in the journal for background.

✿ ✿ ✿

Once there was an arrest, I thought my timeline for writing about Tonya's murder was always going to be contingent on a trial. That went by the wayside once Wells committed suicide, and his death narrowed my focus on the work that still needed to be done to two seemingly straightforward tasks.

The first was to try to find people who were close to Wells and speak with them even though, by all accounts, he was estranged from most of his family except his son, Morgan, who lived in Arizona, and his older sister, Nan, who lived on the same street as him. In the fall and summer of 2020, Nan and I spoke and exchanged text messages, but each time she made it very clear the conversations were off the record. Unfortunately, after quite a bit of back-and-forth, we couldn't agree on what an interview with her might look like or how it might be used afterward. At the end of 2020, Nan moved to Maryland, where one of her sisters lived. I never spoke with Wells' son, Morgan, but I spoke with quite a few people who knew Wells in his day-to-day life. The women he encountered were all scared of him to one degree or another, and the men who knew him thought he was unremarkable, even harmless, and had all been shocked at the news of his arrest.

Going back over the PPD case file, I found several instances where I believe Wells was mentioned early in the investigation, although not by name.

On January 8, 1985, Enterkin interviewed Gary and Michelle Simmons, who were the people Vanita said she saw Tonya talking with when she left Darryl's Bar & Grille with Larry the night of the murder. Gary and Michelle described a tall, thin, blond man in his early 20s who'd been sitting at the bar and who the people in their group thought was acting "suspicious." They said he had a thin nose, wore gold-framed glasses and had a dark suit on. Another woman at Darryl's that night told Enterkin she saw Tonya in the bar with a white male in a suit and tie and said he was "much taller" than Tonya. These two descriptions both seem to be of Wells, but Enterkin was never able to track down the individual.

The last thing I needed to do was find out if Wells' DNA was a match to any of the DNA found on Patricia Stephens, who was murdered two months after Tonya in March 1985. In December 2023, Escambia County Sheriff's Office cold case investigator James Lee confirmed to me it was not a match to Wells, but he said he had two potential suspects in the Stephens murder he was running DNA tests on that month and was trying to get it done before he switched jobs and became a special agent with the FDLE at the beginning of 2024.

A few weeks later, Lee called to tell me the two suspects weren't a match.

Patricia's case remains unsolved.

Tony Adame
Pensacola Beach, Florida
December 31, 2023

APPENDIX

Personal Journal (May 2019–May 2020)

MAY 22-23, 2019

On May 22, Chuck Mallett, the new head of the Pensacola Police Department Criminal Investigations (CI) Unit returned my call from April 19 and asked if I wanted to meet for lunch the next day, and he had something to tell me that I was going to like. But we had to go over a few things first. We met at Jerry's in Pensacola — we both had bacon cheeseburgers with fries and Cokes. He was dressed cleanly — checkered dress shirt, dark slacks, badge and gun. Said he wanted to know why I was looking into Tonya's murder. Gave him the brief spiel, backstory, told him I thought it wasn't fair that she didn't get to raise her son, he didn't get to have a mother. Mallett said he was going to do something he'd never done before. Give me access to all PPD case files, special task force moving forward but didn't want to get "screwed" — he asked that I not write anything or tell anyone about my involvement until the case was solved. "So, you in?" We agreed on one year from that day and shook on it. We began to discuss the case, and he answered several of my biggest questions from the previous five months.

- The DNA recovered at the scene was semen, pubic hair and head hair. All from same person. Semen was in Tonya's vagina and anus. There was also semen, pubic hair and head hair in a towel left by Tonya's body. All of the DNA at the crime scene matched.
- There were dog hairs covering Tonya and in the towel.
- Tim Davidson was cleared through DNA testing several times — Paul Kelly was the last time in 2009, when he took a mouth swab.
- Kurt Lisk had been cleared several times through DNA testing as well. The "old-timers" all were still convinced that Lisk was the killer.
- Jim Enterkin was the first investigator who had the case.
- Paul Kelly is now an investigator with the Florida Department of Law Enforcement.

It seems, from my initial convo with Mallett, that PPD is going to invest a lot of resources — time and money — to making the DNA connection with the same method used to catch the Golden State Killer in California. Mallett also asked me not to tell any of Tonya's family, especially Renee, because of the Facebook page. He tells me I can come by and get copies of the case file and all accompanying stuff at PPD soon. Says it's only two boxes. Mallett ends by telling me, "You filed that records request at just the right time." Mallett thinks it will take two months to solve.

MAY 24, 2019

I went to PPD office at 711 N. Hayne Street to meet with Captain Chuck Mallett, Sergeant Jon Thacker, Lieutenant Adam McCoy and Detective Marcus Savage about Tonya's case. This was the initial group working on Tonya's case. We all met for about an hour, and Mallett gave me the case file and did an initial discussion of the case. They asked me some questions about Tonya's family. The first results from Parabon Nanolabs were about to come back, and we talked about how the case might work as far as building the family tree. All of the work was in response to GSK and how he was caught. Mallett said he'd been told that there was a 4/5 chance that we could solve the case — 1 being an absolute certainty we could solve it and 5 being an absolute certainty we could not. I went home, walked the dog, then spent the rest of the evening looking over the file. I was told that Tonya had a drug arrest that I was not previously aware of and that I needed to come back and get the crime scene photos/other photos from Heintzelman because she needed to go through them to take out the autopsy photos per the Dale Earnhardt Law in Florida.

JUNE 3, 2019

I had to cancel PPD meeting because I was sick — very sick — with stomach ailment. It was awful. Took like a week to shake it. Mallett set up another meeting for 11:30 a.m. on June 12.

JUNE 12, 2019

Went to PPD at 11:30 a.m. to meet with Mallett and McCoy — they had received the first results from the Parabon snapshot of DNA profiles on June 10. There were 4-6 matches that came back, all presumably third cousins, and there were what Parabon described as 3 "good" matches with ties to Northern Florida. They said they were going to decide how to proceed, but the likely process was vetting names on the family tree to get DNA samples that might begin to fill out the family tree some more. They said they used Carolyn Connors, PPD analyst, to do this work. I made a pdf of the entire case file I sent to Mallett and McCoy to pass around. I had to agree to never publish names of anyone who came up in the family tree as a result of Parabon's work — I agreed to this. They explained to me what centimorgans were and how they use them to determine familial relationships. Met with Mallett one-on-one for background info, and he told me about his most memorable case — the Samira Watkins case — she was killed by Zachary Littleton. Samira worked with Mallett's mom, Akiko, at a local McDonald's, so it was a personal case. Met with McCoy and he told me the same — his was about a car chase.

Mallett said he would reach out to Jim Enterkin to see if he would speak with me.

JUNE 19, 2019

Back at PPD to meet with Mallett — this is the first official meeting of the task force to find Tonya's killer. Mallett told me beforehand that Enterkin was a "No" on the interviews. I asked about the initial crime scene supervisor for PPD who oversaw the case and some stuff that was coming up that didn't add up. Mallett said the name of the old CSS was Bob Grant, and "we want to keep Bob Grant out of this." We went to the CI room to have our first meeting as a group — it's a big meeting room with a dozen or so whiteboards all around that have curtains on them. Big table in the middle that was taken over from old PPD offices — has old PPD badges sunk into the corners. This is the room where the PPD works on major cases. In the first meeting were:

- Myself
- Chuck Mallett
- Nicole Heintzelman
- Adam McCoy
- Jon Thacker
- Carolyn Connors

FDLE Genetics/Genealogy Chief Lori Napolitano is also at the meeting via a digital link. Mallett leads the meeting — calls the group the "Gene Team" and starts to talk strategy. The initial thought is to start going after the best connections on the family tree by approaching them and asking for DNA samples — in this case they don't want to contact anyone with local ties in order to keep the investigation secret. We get some good news — because of a lawsuit, they're not going to open any new cases with this method, so FDLE is going to pay for another round of genealogical testing. This is huge — about another $5,000 — they discuss how to approach people. CC will do the vetting to see if it's a good person to approach — several of them are older, and Mallett suggests bringing in his wife, Heather, who also works at PPD, to help approach older people. They identify someone in Texas and plan a trip to go see her. *IMPORTANT THING HAP-PENS HERE.* Mallett addresses one important part of the case — the cops are allowed, legally, to lie to and deceive people when they go approach them for DNA samples. They are legally allowed to concoct a story, and it might benefit them to do so in this case. Mallett tells everyone that he's thought this over and decides that while they need to be very, very careful, they're going to be up-front with everyone they approach, because they don't want to hinder future investigations. If word gets around they're trying to trick people, it might hurt a cop in the future going to get a sample. Mallett emphasizes that they are not reinvestigating the case. Says they will focus specifically on the DNA. Everything else is a distraction (no offense to me).

Talking about the *UNSUB* now — target age is born between 1960 and 1965 (he was born in 1962) and, because Tonya liked older guys, they might stretch that out to 1950. They talk about how important it is to be oh so careful if/when they do close in on a subject. There's a discussion on the price of ancestry kits to give out to people — how expensive they are. Mallett ends the meeting by saying he's going to Tallahassee to drop his daughter off at band camp at FSU the next week and will stop on the way to try to collect DNA from someone we've identified on the family tree. *FAKE NAMES FOR FAMILY TREE?* And that PPD will send someone to Texas in a few weeks.

After the meeting, I went down to the PPD Crime Lab with Heintz-elman to get the crime scene photos minus the autopsy stuff she had to take out. She has an elaborate setup for coffee in her office — with all the different syrups — "I can't have coffee that tastes like coffee" — I like her right away. She worked for Santa Rosa County as a civil-ian, then went to work for PPD in 2001. She showed me all around the lab — there are five full time CS analysts. They work 6 a.m. to 4 p.m. or 4 p.m. to 2 a.m., and there's one flex shift — showed me fingerprint labs, fentanyl, told me about the Nancy Banks case, showed me the evidence locker, which had just been filled with high-grade marijuana.

JUNE 17, 2019

I tracked down Kurt Lisk several days before — he owned a business in Pensacola — one of those weird wind streamers sign businesses

— the ones that stand straight up and are used for car openings or high school football games. Lisk called me back and left a voicemail — I think he thinks I'm someone who wants some business. I called him back and we talked for approx. 10 minutes. He was pretty upset after I told him who I was and what I was calling him about. Said he "wasn't inclined to talk about that" and if he ever changed his mind, he would call me back. I asked him just to stay on the line and listen to questions. He did. He grunted and scoffed several times. I asked him how it affected him — did he know Tonya — was he in a sexual relationship with Tonya — I asked him about that night. He was upset enough that it gave me a bit of a scare. I told Mallett what happened and that I'd decided not to contact him again — or any other suspects for that matter — for fear it might set off some bells on the investigation, etc.

JUNE 26, 2019

Mallett emails the group saying he's made contact with the woman in Texas over the phone, and she's agreed to send in a DNA sample.

JULY 5, 2019

Mallett emails group to say he's made contact with man in Quincy (outside Tallahassee) who agrees to give a DNA sample. All of these are to fill out family tree.

AUG. 16, 2019

Mallett calls meeting to update case and bring in two new people — Kevin Christman is the new head of CI unit while Investigator Danny Harnett is added to the team. Also at the meeting were myself, CC and Adam McCoy. I was able to give the group information on a possible suspect I didn't believe had been cleared through DNA — a man Tonya was with on Dec. 30 and who'd made a surprise move to

Louisiana on Jan. 2. The day after the meeting, Mallett and I meet in his office, and he explains to me that he was the acting head of the PPD while PPD Chief Tommi Lyter was taking care of his sick wife. Mallett had a fancy title, but they decided to shelve it because they weren't sure about repercussions with union etc. so now Mallett is just head of "administration" — a generic do-it-all title that essentially means he's the head of a division ... that just oversees everything I guess. I express to Mallett my fear that now that he's no longer with CI, the case won't get the attention it deserves and he tells me that's just not the case — he trusts Christman and Harnett as much as anyone there, and they both understand that he's still overseeing the case — it's actually the only one he's taking with him as he leaves CI.

On Oct. 18, Mallett sent out an email telling the team that all of the extra samples they'd set out to obtain were collected and the family trees could now be properly filled out. He tentatively scheduled another meeting at PPD for Nov. 20.

NOV. 20, 2019

If there's a low point to the investigation, this might be it. At the meeting were Mallett, McCoy, Heintzelman, Harnett and myself, along with a representative from Parabon on a videoconference call who was going to explain the results from the latest round of genealogical testing and go over the updated family trees. The Parabon rep explained that while the extra DNA samples had done a lot to help fill out the family trees, they'd also added more confusion to the process. The reason for this was the most promising family trees (WHERE THE UNSUB MIGHT BE) had come from Southern Alabama and Northern Florida but that a massive amount of pedigree collapse was occurring between those family trees, and it was making it difficult to identify specific lineages. There was an uncomfortable moment in the room — did we hear that right? Yep. Pedigree collapse is what happens when two individuals who share an ancestor reproduce, which causes the number of the distinct ancestors in the family tree to be smaller. Which also makes them harder to identify. It's also known as inbreeding.

The Parabon rep made it clear this was going to make the task force's work much more difficult and gave us a list of seven names that, if DNA samples could be obtained, could possibly clear up the confusion caused by the pedigree collapse. The task force tried to talk through several solutions of getting around this last hurdle, because all of the names were locals and, up to that point, locals had been off limits. There were no clear alternatives. Mallett, likely sensing the change of mood in the room, tried to spin the dark news from Parabon into a positive. The first 11 months of the investigation Mallett had been, at best, a realist. When optimism flared up on the team early on, he tempered that with hard facts that brought everyone back to earth. Now, he wanted to send it back the other way.

"Look at it this way," Mallett said, "this just means if we find a suspect who has connections to two of these trees, it's either a really great, amazing lead, and we're not far off, or it has a good chance of actually being our suspect."

Mallett also made the decision to turn the heat up a notch in the investigation. Previously, members of the family trees who were locals were not being approached to protect the integrity of the investigation. That day, Mallett said we could begin seeking out possible family members with ties to the area, including several from Pensacola and one from Milton, where Tonya was from.

"And if people start to find out, that's fine," Mallett said. "People do crazy things when they start thinking they're under that type of pressure, so who knows?"

On Dec. 17, Mallett sent an email to the task force stating he'd finished up most of the work on Parabon's to-do list of seven names, and he'd ended up with three good DNA samples out of five people he'd approached and added two more names — and samples — to the list. So five samples total. He'd also decided that several people were too risky to approach. He followed up on something he'd mentioned earlier, in passing — the FDLE was finishing up another case and adding more resources to our case.

Mallett showed me a spare office he'd been using with humongous whiteboards in it — they were all filled up with family trees — it reminded me of the old-timey college classrooms where the professors filled up the chalkboards with formulas. One of the family trees Mallett had traced back to the early 1800s.

"Lori [Napolitano] and FDLE are doing a great job and bringing us leads," Mallett wrote at the end of the Dec. 17 email. "I will let you know when one of them allows us to narrow our focus."

FEB. 10, 2020

Mallett called me shortly before 6 p.m. on Tuesday, Feb. 10. It was our first contact since exchanging greetings around the holidays — so almost 2 months.

"Hey, do you know when Tonya graduated from high school?" he asked me.

I told him she hadn't graduated — she dropped out of high school after the ninth grade but was supposed to be either class of 79 or class of 80 — I thought it was Milton High but Mallett said she'd actually attended Woodham High. Then he told me PPD and FDLE had identified a suspect via family tree research and they were gathering information on him as we spoke.

"The name we've got is Daniel Leonard Wells," Mallett said. "Don't know much else yet except for that he matched up with two family trees. Looks like he's about 57 years old ... born in 1962 and he's from Milton."

The task force's initial guess had been that the UNSUB was born between 1960 and 1965. Tonya, who was from Milton, was born in 1961. We agreed to talk later, and I began frantically trying to find info on Wells.

There was an arrest in 1987 for tampering with a witness in a battery and an arrest in 1989 for solicitation of prostitution — both in Pensacola. I also was able to find out that Wells had been the target of a murder-for-hire plot in Pensacola in 1991 that ended with the wrong man being killed and two men receiving the death penalty. I also found property records for Wells and his family dating back decades in the area. Later that night, I called Mallett and compared notes. That's when I learned that Wells had several arrests for sexual crimes in Missouri and Kansas, including second-degree sexual assault in

Missouri in 1998. Most of the charges seemed centered around the same, repeating act: Wells masturbating in public. Mallett also told me that they'd found a traffic ticket issued to Wells in 1985 when he was living on Elmcrest Street in Pensacola — at the same time as the murder and approximately one mile from where Tonya's body was found.

The DNA phenotype report, which describes physical traits of the unknown suspect, also seemed promising. The report said the suspect had sandy blond or brown hair and green eyes. From his driver's license photo, Wells had green eyes and sandy blond or brown hair. Mallett sent out an email on Feb. 11 saying there would be a meeting of the task force on Feb. 13 in Pensacola.

"We have a suspect to look at. This meeting will catch everyone up and discuss the plan moving forward."

FEB. 13, 2020, THURSDAY

On Feb. 13, I went to PPD offices for possibly the last meeting of the task force. I showed up 30 minutes early to meet privately with Mallett, and we went over some key facts from the timeline of the last year — more for me than for him — and I asked how he planned to tell Tonya's family. His preference was to tell them in person, but he wasn't sure how it was going to all go down. I'd spoken with at least one member of Tonya's family every week for the last 10 months.

In the meeting that day were Mallett, McCoy, Christman, Harnett, Connors, Heintzelman and myself. Mallett began by praising the work of the FDLE and Napolitano, then explained how Wells was the first person they'd found that connected two of the family trees together — what he'd guessed might be the case in the meeting on Nov. 20. Mallett told the room about the phenotype report — sandy blond or brown hair and green eyes. Connors had already started to put together a file on Wells, and it was where most of us were getting out first look at him. Heintzelman asked Connors what color Wells' eyes were.

"Green," she said.

"Well," Heintzelman said, "that might be something."

We also found out Wells' address and that he was 6-foot-6 and about 250 pounds — a huge dude. McCoy, about 6-4 and 275 pounds, heard this and asked if he could be there for the first face-to-face contact with Wells.

Christman said Harnett would begin leading a two-man surveillance team on Wells beginning Monday, Feb. 17, around 6 a.m., and Harnett had already begun using Google maps to look through Wells' neighborhood for possible places to park during surveillance. Someone asked about a "trash rip" — meaning that if Wells placed his trash out on the curb to be picked up, it was fair game to go through and try and pull DNA from. Heintzelman called the county pretending like she was moving to Wells' street to find out when the trash was picked up — Thursday mornings — so we would have to wait a week.

The better plan would be to obtain DNA via surveillance — hopefully, something Wells would discard in public, like a cigarette. Mallett had already begun some surveillance, going by where Wells worked. He said he definitely smoked because he'd seen him buy a pack of cigarettes.

If they could match the DNA off something like a cigarette to the DNA from the crime scene, Mallett said he could obtain a search warrant, go to Wells' home or work to serve it, obtain a cheek swab from him and bring him in for an interview if he was willing. If Wells' DNA from the swab matched the UNSUB, then an arrest could be made. The process of getting the DNA tests could take up to a week, but Mallett felt like in this case the work could be expedited because the FDLE was putting its own resources into the case. "Nothing else has worked on this case like it's supposed to." If it came to an interview, Mallett and Harnett were the ones to interrogate Wells — a prospect that seemed to excite the two of them.

"We're good at it," Mallett said. "We've been doing interrogations for about 20 years together and have good chemistry. But if you don't do it for a while, you get rusty. So if we're going to do it, we need to go over the plan a few times."

I'm told I will be allowed to watch the interview occur in real time, via TV monitors.

"These things can drag on for like 10 hours, so bring some snacks," Mallett said.

A rash of gun violence in the week following the Feb. 13 meeting delayed the surveillance team's efforts to start with. Mallett and I spoke again on Feb. 19, and he told me the FDLE was sending in several agents to help in the next week and that the focus was on obtaining discarded DNA, either via a discarded cigarette or a trash rip.

I also learned more about Wells' sex charges in Missouri — Independence PD had sent over records to Mallett. There were at least a half-dozen reports. We also found out that he'd been married twice and had a son — Morgan — who lived in Arizona.

On Friday, Feb. 28, Mallett informed me that the investigation was going into "full-on mode" thanks to additional manpower from FDLE. On March 4, Mallett called and told me that the surveillance team obtained a discarded cigarette thanks to Harnett that morning.

"This is a very good day," Mallett said. He thought the DNA was being fast-tracked and it would be back to us in less than a week. The next day, FDLE confirmed the DNA obtained from Wells' discarded cigarette was a match to the DNA from the UNSUB in our case.

FRIDAY, MARCH 13, 2020

During dinner with Dr. Joe Patroni and Summer Patroni and their kids at their house on Pensacola Beach — spicy tortellini — Mallett called and told me that the DA decided to skip the search warrant and was going straight to an arrest warrant. There were still some details to be worked out. Mainly over what the charges against Wells were going to be. The onset of the COVID pandemic had started to muck up the machinery a little bit, but Mallett stepped in and effectively said "Hey, I've got a murder case to solve."

SUNDAY, MARCH 15, 2020

Mallett tells me the DA is finalizing the charges against Wells — the debate is between first-degree murder, first-degree sexual battery and they're even considering second-degree murder. I mention what a fuck-you it would be to the investigation and the family if they go with second-degree murder and he somehow gets out of prison one day. Mallett says he won't let it get to that and if he has to, he'll start calling in favors with judges, etc. The next day, Mallett tells me it's going to happen and it'll be first-degree murder and first-degree sexual assault/rape.

TUESDAY, MARCH 17, 2020

Mallett calls me at tennis that afternoon. Tells me more about the judge reading over the case and thinking it was ironclad. Says it's all going down and there's a plan in place to pick Wells up — says to be at PPD by 9 a.m. This is also the same day all the bars and restaurants in Florida were shut down by COVID.

WEDNESDAY, MARCH 18, 2020

I meet Mallett in his office at 9 a.m. — the feeling at PPD is comparable to how it felt on game days in high school and college football — the tension and the excitement. There's been constant surveillance on Wells for the last week. For the first time in that week, he went home from work early — some irony that he did that on what's likely going to be his last day as a free man. Mallett is in a black suit with a white dress shirt and a paisley tie with a wide, Windsor knot. There's a crowd starting to gather in the CI division and outside of Mallett's office as they try to figure out how they're going to bring Wells in to get fingerprinted, and there's some concern that the new fingerprinting machine they have won't work with him because he's too tall, so they say they can do it the old way, which has been pretty much extinct for 20 years (rolling fingers across ink, then the paper) and Mallett's 17-year-old daughter, Maegan/Meagan?, says under her breath, "Commit a murder in the 80s, we'll fingerprint you like it's the 80s," and we all laugh. Mallett and I eat lunch in his office and talk for a few hours about the case — mainly about that day and how it's going to go down. They think there's a good possibility Wells might kill himself, and they know that he sold a gun several years back so they've had to plan the approach very carefully.

At 1 p.m., Mallett and I leave in a black Chevy Traverse we take away from the PPD lot — unmarked car — he's got a gun on him and there's also a black gun in the hand compartment OR does he put the gun in the hand compartment, I can't remember. Mallett and I drive past his job at CDC Woodworking (address) to make sure his truck is still there. There are 3 unmarked cars and 1 marked patrol car with two CI detectives (Osley and Eierhart), acting like they're checking people's speeds. Mallett and I are in one unmarked, Harnett is by himself in another. There are two extra cars available and ready to roll in at a moment's notice. Wells goes into work every day at 6 a.m. and leaves at 3 p.m. We park over one block where we can see the intersection but not CDC Woodworking — one of the unmarked cars is looking directly at the entrance. Harnett is in a black Impala and comes over and we talk for about an hour — he talks about Stephen King and how he wants to write a book, Nicole calls Mallett, then Tommi Lyter calls to go over notes for the press conference the next day. Mallett shows me he's got GOOD bourbon and glasses packed in a camo backpack if things go well.

Mallett says sometimes Wells will bullshit with his co-workers for a little bit before he takes off — at 3:12 p.m., we get the call that he's walking out of the shop — he'll go northbound on Pace Boulevard then west onto Hwy 90 to get home and we'll nab him. My heart is beating out of my chest at this point.

"Danny, you ready to roll out?" Mallett asks him.

The police stop Wells at 3:17 p.m. — he's pulled over by Osley and Eierhart — they tell him because of COVID, they want him to get out of the car and they cuff him right away. Harnett pulls up. All he says is "We need to talk to you about something at the station." Wells says OK. Mallett pulls up behind them and gets out. Wells is tall — he's 6-9 maybe? He's got on a green shirt and camo cargo shorts, gray tennis shoes.

It's a quick ride back to the station — that was the first biggest hurdle to cross. He could've said, "Fuck no," and they would've had to arrest him right there on the spot — spill the whole thing — Osley says Wells was no fuss. Danny says the same thing.

BACK AT THE STATION

There's a big crowd in the CID division — they take Wells in through the back entrance and right into an interrogation room — all that's in the room is a Bible and handcuffs attached to a table.

Mallett, Harnett and Wells begin talking at 3:45 p.m. SEE TRANSCRIPT [chapter 17] FOR EXACT WORDS After about 10 mins of small talk — nothing about the case — just about where he's from and where he's lived — they read him his rights.

They ask him right away if he knew Tonya — nope.

They ask him if he's ever been arrested — nope.

4:35 p.m. — they finally get to New Year's Eve, 1984. Denies living on Elmcrest ... "the name sounds familiar."

4:40 p.m. — "cut to the chase," irrefutable evidence that he was at the scene ... Wells says he's never hurt anyone in his life. "Your DNA is at this site. On this person."

4:55 p.m. — Wells still denying everything — Elmcrest, Collier County — Mallett takes off his jacket — Harnett drops "Ted Bundy" on him.

5:05 p.m. — Mallett says they've sat in this room with monsters. WELLS puts his hands on his face ... "I was with her but I didn't give her a ride home ... Bobby Hicks and Ralph James did."

Wells tries to lie a little bit more ... they tell him not to. "The monster keeps lying."

5:15 p.m. Wells gives full confession — hit her in the head with a cutting board — her friends left her and she needed a ride home — JOHN PENDERGRAST WAS THE ROOMMATE??? 5:15 p.m. Full confession — says they had sex, his friends came over, they left and he wanted to have sex again but she didn't — they argued in kitchen and she slapped him — he hit her on head with cutting board, took her back to bedroom, raped her and strangled her to death.

Wells: "Those were cocaine times. Bad stuff. Alters your sex drive. I hurt her bad. I wanted it to be over with."

Harnett: "Anal?"

Pendergrast had a black Lab. This clears up A LOT of questions over the years — the pets were always a key aspect to the investigation because she had so much dog hair on her.

Wells said they both did coke — this was a lie, or was it — she did not have cocaine in her system. WHAT DRUGS WAS SHE BUSTED FOR?

5:42 p.m. Mallett: "That's how you left her." Shows Wells the pics. "Like a piece of trash." Wells puts his hand over his mouth. Wells asks for water, and Harnett brings him a water.

Mallett leaves to call Timbo and Renee.

6:15 p.m. — Mallett, Harnett, Wells all back in room. Wells says he's relieved. Never told anyone. They want the timeline. Wells admits after he hit her he tried to have sex with her again. She was struggling. He started strangling her again. I BELIEVE HE STRANGLED HER MULTIPLE TIMES.

6:45 p.m. — Mallett/Harnett back in room — We wouldn't be doing our job if we didn't ask about Patty. It's good. You're taking responsibility for it. We'll do our job.

Nicole comes in the room and takes a buccal swab from Wells. Official DNA. Now he's going to be taken to lockup to be booked. Wells says he wants to call his son, Morgan. He wants to call his sister to pick up his truck. For a moment Mallett does the thing with his shoulders. I don't think he's going to let him, but he does.

WELLS: Nan, Nan ... listen. I did something 35 years ago ... I'm at PPD. I committed homicide. They got my DNA ... they've been following me for a while. I've told them. They know what happened a long time ago. I'm accepting responsibility for it ... I should've come clean a long time ago. I'm so sorry. I need to you to get in touch with Morgan, he's going to be getting all of my stuff. There's no bond on it. Tomorrow make first appearance. I love you Nan. I love you. I'm gonna spend the rest of my life in prison.

Call ends at 6:55 p.m.

WELLS then calls "Warren" at his work? "I got arrested ... goes back 35 years ... I did something really bad and I'm not gonna be at work tomorrow ... I'm sure it will be on the news tomorrow ... all the stuff in my shop, give it to my son or Nan."

Nicole comes in to take his fingerprints. They do the perp walk — Danny and Chuck back together again. They put him into the vehicle and walk back. Heather kisses Chuck. Nicole cries. I talk with Chuck and Danny and tell them good job.

We go inside, and the three of us drink an entire bottle of bourbon. Danny asks me how many times I've done this, as a journalist. I say it's my first attempt.

MARCH 19, 2020

Press Conference at PPD

Tonya's family — Renee and son, Tim Jr. — plus all of the old investigative team — Carolynn Stephens, Enterkin — they're brought into the room, and Mallett talks to them. Tells them some details about the day — the presser, about the investigation. Tim drove in from Atlanta. Heintzelman there as well.

Tommi Lyter — PPD Chief: Case passed down from detective to detective, this is a great day for the PPD and the family of Tonya McKinley

Jack Massey — Attorney General/Eddins: Says he'll go after first-degree murder first-degree sexual battery death penalty???

Mayor Grover Robinson: This is not justice denied, it's just justice delayed

MARCH 25, 2020

Phone Call with Mallett

Roommate wasn't John Pendergrast ... it was John Kirtz — Annie Kirtz was his mom — John Kirtz died maybe same day as Tonya ... his obituary was on the same page as Tonya McKinley. Ralph James and Bobby Hicks were dead ends. Kirtz death listed as Jan. 2, 1985.

APRIL 2, 2020

MALLETT CALLS ME AT 6AM — WELLS COMMITS SUICIDE IN HIS CELL — ESCAMBIA COUNTY JAIL

SATURDAY APRIL 4, 2020

Went back into PPD — interviewed Mallett and Carolyn. Found out about what happened with GEDMatch — how we barely got the UNSUB sample in before the pool went from 1 million to 300,000 — we were the last case in the state of Florida and the last case to have access to the 1 million samples before the court case cut that number to 300,000 and everyone had to opt back in. I tell Mallett about the women who have been reaching out to me about Wells.

APRIL 7, 2020

File open-records request through Escambia County for info on sui-cide — get back heavily redacted documents that essentially just say when the call went out to Escambia County Sheriff's office: 4:58 a.m. In a follow-up call to ESCO, I am told by Public Information Officer to stop asking questions about the suicide.

APRIL 20, 2020

Final interviews with Harnett and Heintzelman.

MAY 18, 2020

Celebrated birthday with Joe and Summer Patroni on beach. My plan is to begin transcribing interviews soon.

ACKNOWLEDGMENTS

The research, writing and publication of this book would not have been possible without a large network of people who helped me along the way.

Captain Chuck Mallett of the Pensacola Police Department took a big chance when he decided to bring me into the investigation at its beginning. I didn't realize it at the time, but it was a decision that would end up changing my life. Also at the PPD, Danny Harnett, Carolyn Connors, Nicole Heintzelman and the late Adam McCoy were all tremendous resources throughout this process, as was retired Crime Scene Supervisor Carolynn Stephens.

On Pensacola Beach, a network of friends including Dr. Joe Patroni and Summer Patroni, James Grant, Ashley Johnson and David Sloan, Heather Collins, Sarah Villar, Dr. Bradley Bernard, Mark Stringfellow, Hannah Webb and Jacob Webb made sure I always had a way back to the real world while I was working on this book, and I cherish the time we got to spend together. What a story we will have to tell someday.

My attorney and friend of 30-plus years, Chris O'Hara, was my safety net throughout the entire process. My editor, Deb Gruver, helped shape the book into what it would ultimately become. My agent, Diane Nine, was nothing less than manna from heaven. My nieces, Kyler and Finley, were lifeboats to my sinking ship when I needed it the most. I love you.

Finally, we should all be so lucky to have a sister and a son who love us as much as Tonya's older sister, Renee Ethridge, and her son, Tim Davidson Jr., have loved her. Without their bravery, strength and persistence in the face of years and decades of heartbreak and disappointment, her case would have never been solved.

BIBLIOGRAPHY

Albrecht, Peter. "New Year's Death Unsolved 32 Years Later." WKRG-TV 29 Nov. 2017.

Baker, Blaine. "Play in Rehearsal Judged Best in London." *Pensacola News* 9 Nov. 1979.

Barrows, Mollye. "New Year's Eve Cold Case." WEAR-TV 1 Jan. 2008.

Bradley, Mark. "Second Judge: Death to Bonifay." *Pensacola News Journal* 7 Dec. 1994.

Cawthon, Rod. "Florida's Gulf Coast. ..." *The Washington Post* 3 June 1984.

Chavez, Lorenzo. "Foul Play Suspected in Death of Woman." *Pensacola News* 2 Jan. 1985.

———. "Police Say Woman Died of Strangulation." *Pensacola News* 4 Jan. 1985.

———. "Police Are Seeking Information on Woman Found Dead New Year's." *Pensacola News* 9 Jan. 1985.

"Cold Case Files." "The Clock Strikes Murder." A&E Network/Netflix 25 Feb. 2022.

Dingwall, Bill. "Body Identified as Brent Woman." *Pensacola News Journal* 3 Jan. 1985.

———. "Woman Found Beside Road Died of Strangulation." *Pensacola News Journal* 4 Jan. 1985.

———. "3 Murders Claimed in Phone Calls." *Pensacola News Journal* 6 March 1985.

Foreman Sheppard, Shrona. "Jury Recommends Death for Killer." *Pensacola News Journal* 28 Oct. 1993.

———. "Murder Mastermind Gets Death." *Pensacola News Journal* 25 Jan. 1994.

Fritz, John "Law Agencies Look for Link to Local Deaths." *Pensacola News Journal* 15 Aug. 1991.

Goetsch, Ron. "UWF Initiates Repertory Festival with Two Lillian Hellman Plays." *Pensacola News Journal* 25 July 1980.

Graybiel, Ginny. "Pensacola Man Gets 22 Years for 3 Attacks." *Pensacola News Journal* 24 March 1988.

Hagerty, William H. Jr. "Criminal Psychological Profile: Tonya Ethridge McKinley Homicide." Federal Bureau of Investigation (Jacksonville) 30 Oct. 1985.

Heisig, Eric. "22-year Officer Makes Lieutenant." *Pensacola News Journal* 17 Nov. 2012.

Hiett, Melanie. "Jury Selection Is Today for Trial of Two Charged in Murder." *Pensacola News Journal* 15 July 1991.

———. "Prosecutor: Clark Pleaded for Life Before Fatal Shots." *Pensacola News Journal* 16 July 1991.

National Transportation Safety Board. "Railroad Accident Report: Louisville & Nashville Railroad Company Freight Train Derailment and Puncture of Anhydrous Ammonia Tank Cars at Pensacola Florida November 9, 1977." NTSB 20 July 1978.

———. "Aircraft Incident Report: Boeing 727-235, N47ffNA, Escambia Bay, Pensacola Florida, May 8, 1978." *NTSB* 1981.

"On the Case With Paula Zahn." "New Year's Eve Nightmare." Warner Brothers/HBO Max 18 Dec. 2022.

Pittman Craig, and West, Cindy. "Police Investigate Mysterious Death." *Pensacola News Journal* 2 Jan. 1985.

Richardson, Dave. "Deputies Book 15 on Charges of Solicitation." *Pensacola News Journal* 29 Jan. 1984.

Simmons, Mike. "Pensacola's Finest: The Story of the Pensacola Police Department." Kindle Books Dec. 2020.

Thompson, Sheila. "Body Found Near Millview Road." *Pensacola News Journal* 2 March 1985.

West, Cindy. "TV Show Tries to Solve 1985 Death." *Pensacola News Journal* 6 Nov. 1989.

———. "Four Held in 'Revenge Killing.'" *Pensacola News Journal* 13 Feb. 1991.

———. "Life Full of Questions, Fear for Shooting Victim's Family." *Pensacola News Journal* 13 Feb. 1991.

Staff Report. "Narcotics Arrests." *Pensacola News Journal* 24 Nov. 1975.

—————. "Milton High School Class of 1981." *Pensacola News Journal* 24 May 1981.

—————. "Six Nabbed on Drug Charges." *Pensacola News Journal* 16 Nov. 1981.

—————. "Birth Announcements: Timothy Harley Davidson Jr." *Pensacola News Journal* 27 July 1983.

—————. "Obituaries [Tonya Maria Ethridge]." *Pensacola News Journal* 4 Jan. 1985.

—————. "Crimestoppers: Tonya Ethridge McKinley." *Pensacola News Journal* 12 May 1985, 13 April 1986, 4 Jan. 1987, 15 June 1987, 8 Nov. 1987, 4 July 1988, 23 April 1989, 10 Sept. 1989, 15 April 1990, 13 July 1992.

—————. "Coastal Training Institute Announces Recent Graduates." *Pensacola News Journal* 28 Feb. 1986.

—————. "Police Collar Fugitive in Gainesville." *Pensacola News Journal* 17 Dec. 1987.

—————. "Crimestoppers: Patricia Stephens" *Pensacola News Journal* 5 Feb. 1989, 21 May 1989, 15 October 1989, 12 July 1991, 30 December 1991, 12 September 1992.

—————. "Police Find Chevy Blazer Ditched in Bayou Texar." *Pensacola News Journal* 28 Sept. 1990.

—————. "Pensacola Man Faces Kidnapping, Sex Charges." *Pensacola News Journal* 9 May 1991.

—————. "Divorces: Larry and Vanita Winchester." *Pensacola News Journal* 12 June 1993.

—————. "DUI Arrests: Escambia County." *Pensacola News Journal* 8 June 1994.

—————. "Unsolved Homicides in Escambia and Santa Rosa Counties." *Pensacola News Journal* 24 May 1995.

—————. "DUI Arrests: Escambia County." *Pensacola News Journal* 4 Jan. 1996.

—————. "Bronze Crosses Awarded." *Pensacola News Journal* 19 Feb. 1996.

—————. "Felony Arrests: Escambia County." *Pensacola News Journal* 25 Sept. 1996.

—————. "Felony Arrests: Escambia County." *Pensacola News Journal* 3 June 1997.

—————. "Divorces." *Pensacola News Journal* 7 Aug. 1997.

—————. "Man Drives Car Toward an Officer." *Pensacola News Journal* 29 June 1999.

————————. "DUI Arrests: Escambia County." *Pensacola News Journal* 6 Aug. 2000.

————————. "Obituaries." *Pensacola News Journal* 29 April 2000.

————————. "Unsolved Cases" *Pensacola News Journal* 11 Aug. 2001.

————————. "Obituaries: Rodney Bernard Wells Jr., 1927-2002." *Pensacola News Journal* 2 May 2002.

————————. "DUI Arrests: Santa Rosa County." *Pensacola News Journal* 16 Sept. 2003.

————————. "Escambia Puts Big Face on Unsolved Slayings." *Pensacola News Journal* 25 Aug. 2005.

————————. "Felony Arrests: Escambia County." *Pensacola News Journal* 31 Oct. 2008.

————————. "Obituaries: Timothy D. Davidson." *Pensacola News Journal* 18 Jan. 2013.

————————. "Dissolution of Marriage: Michael Neal McKinley and Tonya Ethridge McKinley." *Pensacola News* 4 July 1984.

————————. "Who Killed Tonya?" *Santa Rosa Press Gazette* 1 Jan. 1989.

————————. "Marriage Applications: Michael Neal McKinley and Tonya Marie Ethridge." *Tampa Tribune* 3 Nov. 1978.

————————. "Fate of Child's Body Debated." *The Baltimore Sun* 30 Oct. 1991.

INDEX

ABOUT THE AUTHOR

Raised in Wichita, Kansas, **Tony Adame** graduated from Southern Oregon University in 2001, where he was a three-year starter on the football team at defensive tackle. After college, he went into a career as a sports journalist and worked for newspapers in Oregon, Kansas, California, Texas and Florida. *Chase the Devil* is his first book.

In 2011 and 2012 his work was honored by the Associated Press Sports Editors Awards. In 2020 he was the writer and host of the Florida Society of News Editors Award-winning podcast and long-form series "The Sheriff: Murder, Lies & Revenge in Okaloosa County."

Adame has appeared on television programs such as "Cold Case Files," "On the Case with Paula Zahn," "Crime Exposé with Nancy O'Dell" and ESPN's "SportsCenter." He currently writes about the NFL for Heavy.com.

www.ingramcontent.com/pod-product-compliance
Lightning Source LLC
Chambersburg PA
CBHW021150160426
42812CB00078B/389